MASTERING THE
"GAME OF SELLING"

MASTERING THE
"GAME OF SELLING"

The Step-by-Step Guide from Prospect
Identification, Negotiation to Closing the Sales

PAWAN KUMAR ARYA

PARTRIDGE

Copyright © 2017 by Pawan Kumar Arya.

ISBN: Softcover 978-1-5437-0021-3
       eBook   978-1-5437-0020-6

All rights reserved. No part of this book may be used or reproduced by any means, graphic, electronic, or mechanical, including photocopying, recording, taping or by any information storage retrieval system without the written permission of the author except in the case of brief quotations embodied in critical articles and reviews.

Because of the dynamic nature of the Internet, any web addresses or links contained in this book may have changed since publication and may no longer be valid. The views expressed in this work are solely those of the author and do not necessarily reflect the views of the publisher, and the publisher hereby disclaims any responsibility for them.

Print information available on the last page.

To order additional copies of this book, contact
Partridge India
000 800 10062 62
orders.india@partridgepublishing.com

www.partridgepublishing.com/india

This book is dedicated to all sales professionals—those who spend day and night in selling goods, products or services for the benefit of human kind.

CONTENTS

Acknowledgements ix
About the Author xi
Preface xiii
Chapter 1:   Game of Selling 1
Chapter 2:   The Sales Process 11
    a)   Sales Personalities 16
Chapter 3:   The Sales Executive 25
    a)   Qualities of Sales Executive 28
    b)   Selling Like an Entrepreneur 42
Chapter 4:   Prospecting: First Step for Sale Journey 53
Chapter 5:   Negotiation: The Key for Closing the Sale 69
Chapter 6:   Closing the Sale with Closing Techniques 79
    a)   Reference Selling 86
Chapter 7:   Goal Setting 89
Chapter 8:   Sharpening the Saw 109
Chapter 9:   Sales Meetings 117
Chapter 10: Art of Introductory Email 125
Chapter 11: Objection Handling in Sales 131
Chapter 12: Pareto Law 139
Chapter 13: Time Management in Selling 145

ACKNOWLEDGEMENTS

I am deeply grateful to my wife, son and parents, whose support, diligent efforts and belief in my dreams have made this book possible.

This book is an outcome of my personal selling experience, the experience I had while identifying the prospects, target segment planning and interacting with the customers during the negotiation process involved in closing the sales. All this has helped in transforming me from an Operations person to a Sales person.

I have spent more than 11 years in Manufacturing & Project Management before moving into sales. I have tried to implement my manufacturing experiences and best practices in the field of sales.

I have passion for sales and destiny brought an opportunity for me to move in sales. I realised that when you work for your passion then your work no longer remains your work, it becomes a part of your life. After moving in sales, I read the best available books on Sales. I came across thousands of prospects to gain the wonderful experience of selling and during this process, I devised the best sale closing techniques.

I am thankful to my sales team & my seniors, whose continuous support and belief in my way of working have fetched the desired results.

I am thankful to all my customers and prospects with the help of whom I learnt and applied my sales techniques.

I wish to express my thanks to those who may have contributed to this work directly and indirectly even though they remain anonymous.

ABOUT THE AUTHOR

Pawan Kumar Arya is BE (Mechanical) and PGDM from Indian Institute of Management (Lucknow). He is having varied experience in Sales, Marketing, Operations and Projects. Before moving on to the sales field, he spent good 11 years in Manufacturing, Operations and Projects at companies like Honda Cars, Case New Holland Tractors and JCB India Ltd. After moving in sales, he created new markets for products, came across thousands of prospects & customers and learnt the art of selling by moving in the field. He believes that you gain real experience when you interact with the customers and negotiate with them for closing the sales. He reads a lot on Sales and gained subject matter expertise by implementing the strategies in the field. In this book, he shares his practical sales closing techniques and strategies in detail. He applied Japanese techniques like Kaizen & Root cause analysis in sales and got great results. The author believes that we all are involved in sales in every field of life, and we negotiate, every moment, with someone at office or at home.

PREFACE

I would like to share my own story; since my childhood I am involved in sales and marketing. I realised my passion for sales in my childhood. At the age of 16 years, I supported my father in his Ayurveda and Unani medicine business. I worked day and night in areas ranging from manufacturing to distribution of Ayurvedic medicines. I did door-to-door sales and promotional activities for Ayurvedic medicines.

I realised that with the sales strategies and marketing initiatives one can increase his business manifold.

I am an avid traveller and love travelling around the world to gain experience of selling and growing markets. I am a firm believer in continuous education.

I am very passionate about sales and meeting the top sales professionals to gain knowledge.

I have read extensively on sales and marketing and attended a number of sales seminars to enhance my knowledge. This book is the outcome of my personal sales experience and the knowledge acquired from reading, seminars, audio courses and personal insights from sales professionals.

I am inviting you all to be a part of my mission to educate and empower sales people. You are most welcome to write back to me with your feedback, suggestions and testimony of this book for value addition in the next reprint.

Mission

My mission is to educate and empower sales people to achieve their personal goals and business targets.

Pawan Kumar Arya

I have created the below declaration for sales professionals. It provides you the power to realise your dreams to achieve your personal goals and professional targets.

Process: Every salesperson should start his day with the following declaration. He has to place one hand on top of the other over his heart with the feeling of voice vibration. Standing in front of a mirror, announce the below mentioned declaration to the world.

Declaration

1. I am an excellent sales professional.
2. I am the best, unique and special.
3. I create my life, and I create and develop my own market for my products.
4. I am flexible, and I am customer-centric.
5. I always achieve my target.
6. I am abundant ... and I attract abundance from all directions.
7. I am awesome
8. I am the best leader for my team.
9. I maintain the best relations with everyone at my home, with my colleagues and my customers.
10. I am the superstar of my field, I am the best.

CHAPTER 1

Game of Selling

MASTERING THE "GAME OF SELLING"

**'Good salespeople are not born.
They're trained.' - Dave Kurlan**

Selling is an art and it starts with the salesman. You can master the game of selling with your attitude, personality, communication skills and knowledge. These characteristics play a major role in selling. The salesman's first impression is like winning half the battle. The first impression is the first step towards long relationship and business with the customer. His personal qualities are the key for selling.

The life of a salesman starts with his tour/visit plan to the prospect site with the dream of closing a sale. The travelling and meeting with the prospects is the lifeline of a salesman.

He is the front face of a company or you can say he plays a driver's role for the organisation's growth.

It is important to understand that Selling is an art. You can excel in the game of Selling by practicing the best sales technique and continuously hone up your skills. The most important part is that one can learn all these by only being in the field and in front of the prospects. For example, one can learn cycling by practicing only in the field, one can learn swimming only in a swimming pool and no one can learn these things by reading books. A salesman converts a prospect into a customer; he uses his selling experience to get a sale by explaining the benefits of the products to the customer. The customer buys a product when he realises that the product will increase his productivity and he will get good return on his investment (ROI). A salesman's role is to add value in the prospect operation.

I analysed that in this world everyone is in the selling business. Every moment you convince someone with your ideas, for example, you convince your wife, kids and colleagues to get things done the way you want and at that time you are selling yourself. At a job interview, you are promoting yourself and selling yourself for a job, for choosing the right life partner you are presenting yourself as the right groom or bride. For daily shopping you are negotiating with the shopkeeper. The selling and negotiation is a part and parcel of everyday life for everyone.

> "If you do not believe in yourself, very few other people will"
>
> – *Anonymous*

Selling is a powerful tool. The economy moves only when transactions happen, when people buy or sell, when people spend and earn. Have you ever analysed the role of selling in economy? How your efforts are helping the economy. The sales people are the backbone of the economy. They are helping companies to sell their products in the market. Also analyse your role as a salesperson in your organisation. How you are contributing to your organisation's growth. You are the engine of your company who keeps the company in motion with day and night efforts. You are the front of your company to build the business. You are generating the requirement of the product for your company.

MASTERING THE "GAME OF SELLING"

In today's economic world, if you are in sales it means you are in the right vehicle. The Sales Department is the heart of a company and the sales team is the blood, which runs the heart smoothly.

Personal selling is a part of everyday life. You sell the product after creating a trust with the customer. You build your reputation with prospects and provide the confidence to the customer in a manner that the customer takes a decision to buy the product. Your role as a salesman is not just selling, it's creating a relationship with the customer and creating a trust in his mind for the product.

Key Factors of Sales:

Brand Value When you are selling a brand then a perceived value is associated with the brand. For example, when someone is buying Apple iPhone or your JCB machine, the perceived value is associated with the brand; you're selling the value associated with brand. People trust the brand they know that an established brand is reliable for a product, service and after sales support. Brand spends money and efforts to establish themselves.

Emotional connect with brand: Companies create an emotional connect with the customer and the customer gets connected with the brand for lifelong. The Harley Davidson customers are so connected with the brand that they tattoo the Harley logo on their bodies. We are always so connected with McDonald's and Coca Cola. Like JCB customers are emotionally connected with the brand they buy (equipment on the name of every family member) and associate themselves with JCB.

Each sale person generates profit to support 12.9 people in company.

Who is generating business - is it sales or marketing? Sales people are the people who interact with the prospect and convert him to a customer. Few people are always confused between sales and marketing.

Marketing: According to the American Marketing Association, 'Marketing is the activity, set of institutions and processes for creating, communicating, delivering and exchanging offerings that have value for customers, clients, partners and society.'

Create your own brand: The companies are creating a brand and selling it worldwide. As a sales professional, you should create your own brand and work on the brand values.

Create your brand according to your leadership style, academic background and sales experience.

In your sales experience, explain about your negotiating skills and how you close the deal; your sales closure rate & your customer relationship management.

Create your identity as a subject matter expert. Start writing a blog or a book on the particular subject in which you are dealing. The book and the blog will provide you the authority to prove yourself as an expert of the particular field.

> Assignment: Write your selling experience. Analyse and realise what's there for you.

Are you born to sell? Identify your passion. If you have a passion to sell, no one can stop you to grow in your career. You should have ability to build trust with your client. Your good listening skills is the key to build a relationship with your customer Everybody appreciates the one who listens and understands first before giving the solutions.

As a salesperson you are independent and should have discipline to work with integrity and honesty.

Successful sales people are resilient and have the ability to listen 'No'. For them, the 'No' means 'next opportunity' and they believe that more the 'No' means more business you can generate.

As a salesperson your role is to create value for the customer. You should listen to the customer very carefully; provide them the solutions. Build a relationship with the customer. People do business with people whom they can trust.

Assignment: Describe the three characteristics of a good salesman.

The power of building relationships in business: People buy from those whom they can trust and as a salesman you should have the capabilities to build relationships with the prospects.

> You need to understand why relationships are so important in selling.

I would like to share a personal story, I visited my hometown last summer for a marriage and to my surprise I forgot my Coat (Jacket) at home. There was no store from where I could buy a good Coat (jacket) for the marriage. I visited one tailor and asked for his help to stitch a good jacket for me. This was festival time and his staff was about to leave. He called one of his master tailors and explained to him that I needed a jacket to wear for a function. He took my measurement and stitched a jacket for me in 5 hours. This situation created a lifelong relationship with that tailor. By doing something extra for your customer you win them for life.

R selling: You definitely heard eselling, Internet selling and I am sure you never heard R selling. R selling is relationship selling. You build relationships with customers and they will buy from you only. Building relationships with the customer is easy. You need to just follow very simple things. Greet your customers on their happy birthday and anniversary. Write a note of thanks after meeting the customer. Thank them for their references and feedback. Solve their issues or address their concerns regarding your product and take prompt action in case of any product issue.

This small thing will help you build long-term relationship with your customer and differentiate you from other companies' salespersons. The best way to build relationships is to under promise and over deliver. For example, a customer asks for delivery on a particular day, you must ensure the delivery of the product on the required day and time or try to deliver one day in advance. It will be helpful for building trust on the very first day of product delivery.

Eselling: Another name of Eselling is Emotional selling. The recent study proves that people buy product based on their emotions and feelings and later, they provide logic to justify the purchase by facts and figures. As a salesperson you need to connect the product features with the customer pain areas and win the customer emotionally with benefits. You don't need to force or push the product, you need to listen to the prospect with due attention and create the caring image for the prospect. For the Emotional selling, the basic mantra is to convince the customer with positive features and benefits he will get from the product. Your approach should be solution and value-driven in place of pricing or sales-driven. For example, for selling an insurance policy the emotional connect will be taking care of a family, how a person's wife feels when he secures their future. You can sell any product if you connect emotionally with them.

CHAPTER 2

The Sales Process

MASTERING THE "GAME OF SELLING"

The Selling process is a step-by-step approach for identifying a customer's needs and requirements. It involves providing the solution to value addition in customer processes. The selling process plays a very important role in closing the sales.

In the Selling process, first, the salesperson needs to analyse his customer's profile. After accessing the customer, the salesperson submits the quote and convince the customer with his sales presentation. After the sales presentation, the customer clarifies his doubts and negotiation process starts. The negotiation process takes us towards the closing of the case.

The salesperson should be prepared and know the required technical knowledge before approaching a customer. His preparations will provide him the confidence level and will create a brand image.

Now, let's understand the official definition of sales.

What is Sales: A sale is the exchange of a commodity or money as the price of a good or a service. Sales is an activity related to selling or the amount of goods or services sold in a given time period.

I believe that sale is not only restricted to the definition. It is the start of a relationship between the buyer and the seller. A salesman's responsibility is to add value to prospects' lives by selling his product, and I personally believe that a salesman's responsibility starts after the sale happens. He is responsible for the product delivery, installation and after-sale support. He should create a bonding/relationship with the customer for future sales or references.

> To be what we are, and to become what we are capable of becoming, is the only real end of Life.
>
> -Robert Louis Stevenson

MASTERING THE "GAME OF SELLING"

Let's understand the differences between Sales and Marketing:

Sales	Marketing
1) In a Sales process, we identify our target prospects and approach them.	1) In marketing, we create the brand with the help of 4 Ps of marketing strategy. Product Place Promotion Price
2) Sales is a one-to-one process to identify the customer needs and problems and provide the solutions and products based on his requirements.	2) In marketing, the message is provided to many customers through advertising, customer meetings, sales promotion and branding activities.

We can do better in sales, if we understand about the sales personalities and how they can impact the sales. You can make a judgement and make your own action plan to be a better salesperson.

Sales Personalities

In one of the recent articles published in Harvard Business Review they defined about 8 types of sales personalities.

As per the research, only 9.1 % of the sales executives meet results in sales. They analysed and found out that only 1 out of 250 salesmen exceeded their target.

The research explained that how 8 different types of sales people perform?

1) Experts: 9 % of the sales people come under expert category. They are all-rounders and have the required characteristics and passion for sales. They are equipped with required skills.

2) Closers: 13% of the sales executives considered as closers. Their talking style is smooth and they have the required expertise for sales closing.

3) **Consultants:** 15% of sales executives work like consultants. They have required listening and problem solving skills. It's observed that they are not pushing sales to full potential.

4) Sales architect: 63% of sales people come under the sales architect role. They develop the market; they provide the required awareness of the product.

5) **Storyteller:** This kind of sales people are customer-focused and love case studies. They have focused meeting agenda. They share product features and need to work on listening skills.

6) Narrators: They rely heavily on marketing material. They come up short on challenging questions.

7) Aggressors: They focus on price negotiations. They are aggressive on getting orders.

8) Socialisers: They make friends instead of deals. They need guidance on how to convert chitchat into sales closing.

Exercise: Identify your sales personality?

Write an action plan to be an Expert?

In this chapter, we will discuss the journey of the sales process.

The classification of customers is as follows:

1) Retail customer: Retail customers are either using the product for their own use or for hiring business.
2) Big corporate: Big corporates are the companies which are working on major projects or getting government contracts. Their requirements are big as compared to retail prospects. The corporate sales grow based on the relationship building with major clients. They need special attention in terms of sales & services. The corporates have big presence geographically. They will provide the big platform for your products. The products with corporates create the brand image of the products for retail buyers.

After understanding your prospects' requirements, convert them into loyal customers by the following steps:

1) Customer needs: First understand the customer needs and requirements and provide them the right solution.
2) Presentation on products: Provide the complete product knowledge to the prospect through your presentation and brochure.
3) Quote submission: Submit the quote to the prospect with the required product details.
4) Reference of existing customers: Provide the reference of existing happy customers to create a positive image of your product and services.
5) Ask for an order: The last and important process of sales is to ask for an order.

Clarification on customer objections: During your sales process you will come across various objections from your customer. You have to provide the right answers for all the objections raised by your prospect. The prospect will provide you an order once all his objections and queries are resolved.

Exercise: Write your most common objections and prepare your response in advance. The study says that for every product the most common objections will be maximum 5 in numbers.

Most Common Objection for My Product		
Objection handling worksheet		
Objection	My Response	Remarks

Solution for funding/financing the product: As soon as you close the order from the customer, the next step is to provide them with the right financing solution.

Analysis of your meeting: After each meeting, you need to analyse the meeting with the following exercise. I won the customer or I lost the customer: If I won the customer then I also need to analyse the process. If I lost the customer due to competition then I also need to analyse why I lost the business. Is it only the pricing/cost of the product, Is it due to bad reference or is it due to after-sales support.

Exercise:

A) What did I do right?

B) What would I do differently?

What Do the Sales Statistcis Say

Follow Up : Follow up is required in sales. In Sales, 48% of sales people never follow up with a prospect and they lose the customer to competition. While, 25% people make a second contact and stop follow up and wait that the customer will call back for order; 12% people make a third contact and stop following. Only 10% of sales people contact the same customer more than three times. Now, the sales statistics results are really interesting. Only 2% sales are made in first contact, 3% sales on second contact, 5% sales on third contact, 10% sales are made on fourth contact and 80% of the sales are made on the 5th–12th contact.

Sales Statistics

48% of Sales People Never Follow Up With a Prospect

25% of Sales People Make a Second Contact and Stop

12% of Sales People Only Make Three Contacts and Stop

Only 10% of Sales People Make More Than Three Contacts

2% of Sales are Made on the First Contact

3% of Sales are Made on the Second Contact

5% of Sales are Made on the Third Contact

10% of Sales are Made on the Fourth Contact

80% of Sales are Made on the Fifth to Twelfth Contact

Trust: Trust is very important in the selling process. Customer buys the product or services when he is having trust on you first and then in the company. And, then he trusts the product and makes the final buying decision.

Credibility: The salesman needs to develop the credibility with the prospect. His credibility provides the confidence to the prospect in the product and company.

Presentation: How a salesman gives the presentation to the customer creates the base for the product's future. The effective presentation will create the solid foundation for the product.

Kaizen in selling process: Kaizen is Japanese philosophy. Kai means change and Zen means for the better. Kaizen means for the better. Kaizen is a very important part in Japanese manufacturing process. I believe we can apply Kaizen technique in sales in a much better way. You need to make some improvement in your selling process on daily basis. Kaizen is way of life and it should be applied in sales process. I personally applied Kaizen for my sales journey. Every day I am applying one Kaizen technique in my selling process. With the help of daily Kaizen, my sales process has improved, customer satisfaction has increased and credibility has increased manifold.

I have also applied another manufacturing technique in sales, i.e., Root cause analysis. After every loss in sale, I apply the Root cause analysis for the same.

Why I lost this sale: You need to think over it that why your competition got the order, what are the positives and negatives about the competition product.

Is it due to Price/Quality/Delivery/Model. Why our price is more? You should have justification for your price. Your product provides more value to the customer with respect to price. People are always ready to pay for the product if it's providing high value to them.

I would like to share a story, that people are ready to spend huge money if you can provide the solution to their problems.

One sales executive from India went to Canada and joined the job of sales at the biggest departmental store. On the very first day of his job, he did his work with great interest and passion. At the end of the day, the head of the departmental store asked him about how many customers he attended on that day and what his sales count was. The Indian salesman said, 'Sir, I attended one customer and closed one sale with him.' Boss got angry and said one sale in a day. You know every salesman here is doing 20 sales on an average.

Boss: Okay, tell me what you sold and the collections from sales.

Indian Salesman: Sir, the total collection is £ 935,000.

Boss got surprised and asked how he did it.

Then the Indian salesman explained: Sir, today one customer came and firstly sold him one fishing small hook, then medium and one big hook. Then I sold him one fishing rod and few fish gear. Then I asked him where will he go to do fishing. He said that I will do it in the coastal area. Then I recommended him one boat and sold him one boat from our boat section. Then, I asked him about his vehicle and recommended him that he cannot carry the boat in his Volkswagen, he should buy a right vehicle to carry the boat. I took him to our automobile section and sold him one 4x4 Deluxe Blazer.

The surprised boss asked him that you sold all these things to one customer who just came for one fishing hook. The salesman replied, no sir, he came here for headache pills and I suggested him that pills are not good, you start fishing and that will release your headache issue.

MASTERING THE "GAME OF SELLING"

Exercise: You need to identify your target customer, decision makers and good reference to win the sales order.

- **Who Is my Target Customer?**
- **Who is the Decision Maker?**
- **Who can Provide Reference?**

CHAPTER 3

The Sales Executive

MASTERING THE "GAME OF SELLING"

The salesman starts his career with the profile of Sales Executive...moving in the field...door to door, office to office and generate prospects or find the customers for his product.

I also started my journey as a sales engineer for industrial lubricant. After my Diploma in Automobile Engineering, the first job I got was of a Sales Engineer. My role was to sell industrial lubricants in the industrial areas of Delhi and NCR. I used to travel industry to industry to explain about the products - the benefits vs competition. Few organisations are very price savvy. They don't want to buy the costly product and you need to convince them about the quality and value you are providing in your product. During this phase of moving from door–to-door sales, I learned a lot about human psychology - why and when people buy.

I realised that the most valuable asset as a salesman is your attitude, your smile while meeting with customers or any one you are dealing with. Your ability to listen to the customer and then helping them with the right solution makes all the difference.

Monday is the starting day and you think that you will achieve your target in the week. But moving from prospect to prospect for getting the final order requires lot of efforts and courage.

I would like to share my personal experience, I did not do any sales in the first six months and realised that you need to focus on specific target segments and customers. You cannot sell to the entire world.

I realised the value of continuing education and invested in my education for learning new skills.

I also realised that if you believe in your product, you can convince the customer in a better manner for making the product selection.

How many of you are enthusiastic about your profession? You need to have passion for what you do, you should love what you do, people will say yes to your belief and your confidence in the product.

I could not sell till I believed it was good for the consumer.

Belief: Your belief in you will create the difference, your belief in your company and product will define your journey.

Good Talkers: Are you required to be a good talker to achieve your sale?

Qualified People to sell: To whom you are going to sell. The target audience is qualified enough to understand the need and value of the product. You need to help people to make good decisions for themselves.

Always ask such questions whereby the customer is forced to provide an affirmative reply to at least one of them. Always give them two questions. Answers must confirm the decision to go ahead.

e.g., Mr Nitin, can we meet today at 3:00pm or tomorrow morning at 9:00 am?

Qualities of Sales Executive

I am going to share with you the mantra to be an excellent and successful sales manager in your career.

You need to develop the following qualities to be an icon in your organisation:

1) Physical appearance

The salesman's knowledge and personality plays a very important role in closing the sale. The salesman should be in the right uniform and clean shaven or with right beard to look like a sales executive. The first impression is the last impression in the field of Sales. The customer judges the company and the product based on the salesman's personality and the way he speaks with the customer.

2) Reputation and credibility

A salesperson's reputation is the most valuable asset. He should develop his reputation as a successful professional. At last, people don't care how much you know until they know how much you care about them. You need to build your credibility with every prospect in the field.

3) Product knowledge

The salesman should be thorough with his product knowledge. He should be aware about the complete technical details of the product. He should be aware of the complete knowhow about the technical brochure he is submitting to the prospect. Knowledge of the product and knowledge of the competition is the key mantra for success.

The salesperson should first understand the customer requirement and then provide the solution to the customer with his product and services. An analysis is required for providing the right solution to the customer, including:

A. **Product Knowledge**

   a) Feature
   b) Function
   c) Benefits
   d) Safety

B. Industry Knowledge: The knowledge of industry is required; you should know what competition is offering. What's the size of the industry? What's your market share? Who is leading the industry in that segment, etc.

C. Pricing Knowledge: The sales executive should know the product pricing, the competition product pricing and product positioning with respect to pricing.

D. Application Knowledge: The product applications and the way customer can get the benefits. The multiple applications your product can perform. All these are required to share with your prospects during positioning your product as the right product for him.

E. Competition Knowledge: You should know about the complete details of the competition products, the positives and negatives in the available product range. If you have thorough knowledge about the competition then only you can pitch your product with the right strategy.

4) **Polish your soft skills**

He should also be familiar about the soft skills like how to introduce himself to the prospects, how to ask for permission for meeting and product presentation. The most important part is how to handle the queries. The salesman is not representing himself; he is actually representing his company. He is the first face of the company to the customer. The customer creates the image of the company based on the interaction done with the saleperson. The sales executive's personality impacts the customer's mind.

5) Self-confidence

The salesman's self-confidence plays a very important role. While visiting and meeting with the customer he should be self-confident. He should confidently give the product presentation and features to the prospect. His confidence level convinces the customer about the product and company. The salesman should work to develop his self-confidence. The confidence level will reflect in his personality. It will also provide you the power to persuade the customer for your product and for closing the sale faster.

6) Honesty

His intention should always be to resolve the customer concern, and he should be honest with the customer about the product capacity and deliverable. He should not overcommit to customer about the product. Being honest is the key mantra for sales executive. It will create a brand for the sale executive and the organisation. Honesty is the best policy in the long run. If you are honest while dealing with customers and prospects, it will create a long-term association with the customer.

7) Attitude and motivation

The salesperson should be self-motivated and ambitious. He should be goal-oriented and have passion for sale. He should have a burning desire to excel in the field of Sales. Your positive attitude will say a thousand words. Your attitude will decide your altitude in sales. Your attitude will take you to the pinnacle of sales career.

8) **Patience & persistence**

Patience is of utmost important in sales. Every sale process takes time and we cannot push the sales as per our need. We have to provide sufficient time to prospect for planning and placing the order. We need to understand the situation. Sometimes under pressure, the salesman pushes too hard for closing and it irritates to customer and he will simply deny you. Few customers are critical and you need to be patient with them. One should handle all the customers with respect and patience. Develop unshakable persistence, resolve in advance that you will never give up until you are a big success in your sales career.

The famous story of bamboo tree teaches us the power of patience and persistence.

When you plant a bamboo tree you need to nurture the plant like other plants with right quantity of water, soil & fertilizers. In the first year, you take care of the tree with regular water and fertilizers, but you will not find any visible growth sign. In the second year, again you work hard with regular watering, sunshine and soil, but you will not find any result of growth. The farmers again work hard for third and fourth year with regular watering, fertilizers and take care of plantation. But no growth is visible on the surface. In the fifth year, a small growth will appear and to the surprise of all 80 feet tall bamboo tree emerges. This teaches us the power of patience and persistance. Sometimes, we would like to quit and like to start something new. But the bamboo tree story teaches us that you have to keep the patience and wait for the right time. Your efforts will be rewarded.

The Chinese Bamboo Tree grows 80 feet tall in just six weeks!

Have you ever thought that really Bamboo tree grows only in the fifth year. We need to analyse that what happened in first four years. During the first four years, the tree was growing inside, it was working on the roots to remain strong enough to sustain the pressure of height. If the tree root system will be weak it cannot support its height.

If you would like to achieve big in life, you need to work hard for your dreams without doubting on the system and efforts. Your efforts will create the fruits for you.

To achieve big success in life you have to work hard patiently and keep moving with a positive attitude.

> *Keep Yourself Positive,*
> *Cheerful and Goal-Oriented.*
> *Sales Success is 80% ATTITUDE*
> *and only 20% APTITUDE.*
> *— Brian Tracy*

9) **Handling of rejection**
Sale is rejection business. As per 80/20 law, you get 20% success while meeting with 100 prospects. Do not take any rejection personally. It is the customer requirement that he is buying or not. It is not your fault that the product is not selling. Every 'No' in sales means look out for the next opportunity. Every salesman should analyse each of his every meetings for improvement. He should analyse what he did right or wrong after the meeting and find out the areas of improvement for his next meeting.

10) **Passion for selling**
You have to be passionate about your selling profession. Put your 100% in each sales call. Your 100% in each meeting, each presentation and dedication towards your product and company will show you the path to success.

11) **Sell like a real professional representing a company**
In each sales call, your motivation and enthusiasm should be like that you are the head of your company. Your confidence level should be at the highest level. Your way of representation and communication with the customer should be like a real professional.

12) **Prepare before meeting**
Prepare yourself before every meeting. Before meeting a prospect check about his business, his requirement, his operation and the needs. Prepare your presentation and product pitch before the meeting and reach the customer site before the scheduled time.

13) **Dedicate yourself for lifelong learning**
    The key mantra for success in life is continuous learning. Learn something new on a daily basis. The day you stop learning your growth will start stagnating from that day. Always read books on Sales and watch videos and listen to audio books of successful sales professionals.

14) **Build on relationship and networking**
    Always build long-term relationship with your customers. Always support them for required service. Provide them the right solution. Suggest them the right product. Do the value addition in their processes. Solve their problems. Always be fair with the customer. Always show empathy to your customer. Build good relationship and develop your network as a reliable sales professional.

15) **Objection handling**
    Objection handling is the key to close the sales. Handle customer objections very carefully. Always be prepared for the customer objections with the right justifications and action plan.

16) **Sales prospecting**
    For every sales professional the prospecting is the key for growth and regular sales. The sales funnel should be full with prospects. Always do every activity for prospecting.

17) **Cold calling**
    Ensure cold calling for finding the right target audience. There should be no phone fear, no fear of rejection. The cold calling is just the process for finding the right prospect for your product. It is the way to reach out to the target audience.

18) **Dealing with product, pricing & positioning**
Deal with the customer about pricing in such a manner that you are providing more values as compared to product pricing. Convince the customer that your product will deliver the maximum returns for his investment. People are always ready to pay higher price for product reliability, quality and services. No one is looking for cheap or low cost product. Pricing is the part of closing the sale. If you convince to customer that pricing is appropriate with respect to values then he will always be ready to pay. Always position your product as the best product available in the market.

19) **Territory planning or area coverage**
The most important part for sales executive is to know how to cover his territory for full coverage. Always plan your travel for maximum effectiveness. If you are going to meet someone in one side of your territory then plan for all maximum meetings in that particular area. It will increase your effectiveness. If you cover your territory well then there are tremendous chances that your business will grow multiple times.

20) **Goal setting and time management**
You should always do goal setting for your professional and personal life. The goal setting and time management will provide you unbelievable results. You can achieve multiple times with your goal setting and time management.

21) **Enthusiasm**
The salesman's enthusiasm is the key for getting the order. How enthusiastic are you in selling will determine your success rate.

Norman Vincent Peale: State of Your Enthusiasm

> "If you are not getting as much from life as you want, then examine the state of your enthusiasm"
>
> — Norman Vincent Peale

Zig Ziglar: Penicillin Out of Moldy Bread

> "If man can make Penicillin out of moldy bread, just think about what you can do with yourself"
>
> – *Zig Ziglar*

The butterfly story teaches us a big lesson in life. Like the butterfly, a salesperson needs to evolve and pass through various stages of sales process to become a successful professional in life.

The butterfly evolves from a cocoon; a very small aperture opens up in the cocoon and little butterfly struggles for hours to come out from very small hole. During this natural process of hard work, the fluid circulated in the wings and legs of butterfly and gives the required power to the butterfly to fly as soon as it get free from cocoon. If someone helps the butterfly to come out from the cocoon without so much struggle and pain then the required blood will not circulate from the wings and legs of the butterfly and the butterfly will spend his whole life crawling around. The butterfly body will not look good and it will be having swollen body and shriveled wings.

Struggle provides us the power to fly, the life obstacles and hurdles give us the learning to grow. To be successful in your professional and personal life, one has to cross various struggles in life.

'There is no failure except in no longer trying. There is no defeat except from within, no really insurmountable barrier except for our own inherent weakness of purpose.' - Elebert Hubbard

> For every sale you miss because you're too enthusiastic,
>
> you will miss a hundred because you're not enthusiastic enough.

Take Away:

1. The salesperson should make a resolution that he will become the best salesperson in the industry. He needs to start his day early with planning and putting extra efforts than other salesman.

2. The salesperson should have a target of calling 100 prospects every week. There should be no phone fear.

3. Accept 100% responsibility for your work and your life, and refuse to make excuses for any reason.

4. Each salesman should take own responsibility for his personality and educational development.

5. Take pride in selling and provide the value to your customers. When you add value to the customer pain areas you will also feel important yourself.

6. Think and act long term for your sales career, and in your life.

Exercise

The Sales Executive should self-evaluate himself on the learnings from this chapter: Customer buys product for the solution. They are looking for value addition in their process.

You need to write your answer for the following questions:

Q 1: I like sales because....

Q 2: Write your plan for prospecting:

Q 3: Write your target segments

Q 4: I like my company because....

Q 5: My success % in closing the sales is....

Q 6: In the sales field, travelling is....

Q 7: In my sales career, I see myself as....

Selling Like an Entrepreneur

*'Build a better mousetrap and they will beat a
path to your door' - Ralph Waldo Emerson*

What comes in your mind, when we say Entrepreneur: Is he a job creator, risk taker, visionary, passionate, and strategic & hungry for success. How an entrepreneurial selling is different from professional sale process. It's a unique process of selling. An entrepreneur is having limited resources. The entrepreneurs are having very narrow foundation. The pyramid is turned upside down.

What defines a Salesperson? What characteristics come in your mind when you think for a salesperson? Think about the characteristics associated with salesperson? A salesperson has the backup of Company, Marketing & Service facilities. They have marketing material. They are having the required infrastructure and marketing material. The salesman should have entrepreneurial qualities. Entrepreneur is a person who grows on his own with limited resources. He is having passion for his product and desire to capture the market with his own efforts.

They have to do everything on their own. Characteristics of an Entrepreneur Seller are as follows:

1. Charismatic: I have observed that an entrepreneur has a charismatic personality and self-driven motivation. They have passion for what they are doing.
2. Knowledgeable: They have required knowledge for the product and market. They know where is the demand-supply gap, how they can pitch for their product in the market.

3. Hardworking: No one can replace the hard work. The hard work is the key to success. Key to entrepreneurship is hard work.
4. Care for people: They believe in Win Win ... They have a problem solving approach. They care for the customer and their team members.

The entrepreneurial selling process is having three phases. Let's understand the relationship between them

Preparation Phase	Execution Phase	Analysis Phase
Target Audience	Engaging Lead Generation Qualifying	Relationship Management
	Making the match Proposing Determining Proposing	Measurement
	Doing the deal Closing Re-selling Expectation	

Preparation Phase: In preparation phase, they work on target audience. Who are their target prospects? They work very closely and with target customer to prove their product and establish themselves in the market as a startup. The following steps are to be considered during their preparation phase:

Filtered Target List: They prepare very focus-filtered target list sometimes. We start too broad that delude ourselves.

Art of Sales Conversation: They are always ready for sales conversation. They follow the forward and reverse gear process, as soon as they observed any opportunity to sell, they put their system in first gear with a moment' notice. For example, whenever they visit any party or networking event they start with small talk in a natural way. With every potential prospect they introduce themselves and with message that it is really nice to meet you, if the conversation is not going in the right direction they opt for reverse gear. High-performance sales people always talk about the product or service they are selling.

Follow up: After the meeting they believe in follow up with the target prospect.

The entreprenur selling process includes the following:

1) Prospecting Script: They are always ready with prospecting script. Even if they are on the phone they are ready with sale script.
2) Art of Introductory Email: They believe introductory email is the most important selling tool. They follow this tool regularly and religiously.
3) Qualifying Questions: They are ready with qualifying questions, to identify the prospect requirement.
4) Impact Question Checklist: They have good impact questions. These impact questions will create the requirement of their product in customer mind.

5) Objection List: They religiously work on customer objection list and ready with strong reply on the customer objections.
6) Proposal: They submit the proposal after each meeting.
7) Story Matrix: They have the best story to capture the customer.

I interviewed one of the entrepreneurs and asked: What is most important in sales? He replied, 'What I believe that sales start from you. The most important is YOU. People buy from you.' They firstly believe in you before anything else. You are the first contact point that creates the product awareness; explain to them about the product utilisation. You are the front face of organisation. You have to believe in you. Your self-belief creates the success story in sales.

Second most important thing is WHY? The second most important in sales is Why? Why people buy your product. Your product should create the value to customer. You need to understand the power of asking questions. Selling is hard when you don't know how?

Following are the qualities of a top entrepreneur, who excel in selling their products:

1 Ambitious: They are very ambitious. They are in to 20%. The top 20% people will make 80% of the sales. You need to understand they start with bottom and reach to the top. If you are struggling you need to upgrade your skills.

2 Fear: They believe that fear is single obstacle in their way to success, the fear of rejection. They assume always 'GO' for 'NO'. For them No is the next opportunity. The more no you can trigger by asking for your product or services, your chances of success is very high. One entrepreneur shared a success story of rejection with me, they started one competition that who will get the maximum numbers of NO. At the end of the month, the person who collects the maximum NO is the winner and will be awarded with prize. To the surprise of all, the person who wins maximum No from clients achieved the maximum sales in that month.

Rule: In order to get rid of fear, do the things you fear and the death of fear is certain. Call 100 people and ask for an appointment.

3. Commitment to success: They are committed to success, they firmly believe in The Pareto Law that 20% of the people make 80% of the money. Successful people make 100% commitment to be successful. What is the one actionable step you take today? Keep yourself Positive. Sale process is 80% attitude and 20% aptitude.

One of the successful sales professionals shared the following:

1. Never allow your prospect to lead: You need to lead the conversation with your prospect. The best way to control is that the prospect should ask relevant question.

2. Pre-meeting research: Never neglect the pre-meeting research. Spend some time to research about the prospect. I learned this lesson the hard way. I did not spend time to understand about the company and what they are doing. Invest time to learn about your prospect.

3. Too much talking: Most of the sales executives talk a lot during the sales presentations. Engage with the prospect by asking questions.

4. Irrelevant information: Don't provide irrelevant information to the client during the meeting. Prospects are interested only in how the product is beneficial to them.

5. Unprepared for sales presentation: Always be prepared for the sales presentation. Always be ready with brochure and technical details. Make a checklist so that you have all the required information.

6. Fail to ask for sales: Always ask for sale in a cheerful manner. Even seasoned sales professionals make the mistake.

'Keep yourself positive, cheerful and goal-oriented. Sales success is 80% attitude and only 20% aptitude.'

Which closing strategy works best for you and why?

How to become a highly paid sales professional: If you don't make decision to be in top 20% automatically you will be in the remaining average 80%. The vital key to be in top 20% is that top sales people love their sales profession. You have to be excellent in your sales profession. Everybody who is today at top 10% start with the bottom 10%. They do exactly what they want. According to the research only 3% have written goals and they are most successful. Write down your goals at the first place. Back your goals with word power. Resolve that nothing can stop and discourage.

Lifelong learning: You have to be committed to lifelong learning. Attend seminar and listen to audio programmes. Become a valuable salesperson in your company. Top sales people use their time well. How you spend your time determines your destiny.

Follow the leaders: Do what the top sales people do. Follow the leader and do not follow the follower. Go to the top and ask for advice. Enquire about their attitude and philosophy. Know that the character is everything: Guard your integrity. You must have credibility. The people should trust you and believe in you.

Inborn creativity: Take yourself as a highly creative person. I am a Genius. The fact is that every person has the ability to perform at genius level in one or two areas. Practice the golden rule: Think about yourself as a customer. How you want to be treated as a customer.

Pay the price of success in advance: They start little earlier. They work hard and always are passionate. If you want to become financialy free and successful sales professional work on these ideas.

Should you be in sales? Have you analysed yourself that you should be in sales or not?

Why and how people buy? Is that how you are approaching in the Game of selling?

Sales is when you hit your target you get more commission and more money? You can change your destiny in sales.

Four things to readjust your mindset are as follows:

1. Is it natural or nurture: By sales benchmark index that 13% sales people are natural born sales people and remaining 87% need to work on their skill set. A study shows that one of the 9 people employed in the sales profession in the United States is a natural salesperson and other 8 people have to nurture their skills to become a successful sales professional.

Do you love what you are selling? You need to love your product. Should you love what you are selling? You should love what it will do for your customer. You should like your product and should have a convincing power to convince your customer that your product will increase the productivity of the customer and reduce their cost.

2) Do you need sales process; Most of the people never close their sales because they are not having the sales process. Most of the companies are not having sales process. One study shows that when you have written SOP-standard operating procedure then your sales will increase by 48%.

3) Sale process is too rigid. I understand that sales process is too rigid. These will work if you follow the system. Add what is unique to you & absorb what is useful. Discard what you find is not good for sales. You can redefine your own sales process.

4) Own Personal KPI: Measure yourself what is your own key performance indicator (KPI)? What is your closing rate? What is your average order size? What is your sales cycle? Find your own sales KPI.

What makes great sales people great: They understand that self-motivation is necessary. The great people know that motivation come from themselves. They have to be very clear for their purpose and know why they are doing it? Self-motivation is an inside job. Self-management is a capacity to be accountable and capacity to deliver.

They should have the following skills:

Burning desire to make it happen: Desire to sell! Desire to excel, love for selling is required to be a great salesperson. Lots of sales people are reluctant and hesitant in meeting people. Need-based selling is dead nowadays, customers buy when they want. This is the secret of 21st century sales. Personal skills are the multiplier. You need to work hard on yourself. The following process will help you achieve 93% success rate.

1 Job Skills: Every sales manager should have required job skills, Should have thorough Product Knowledge, industry knowledge and competition.

2 Sales Skills: You should educate yourself with sales skills.

3 Prospecting skills: You should learn how to prospect.

4 Questing skills: Learn the art of asking and replying questions.

The secret skill is personal skill: The secret to excel in selling depends on your personal ability to sell and deliver. The goal setting and self-motivation plays an important role for achieving the targets. Measure yourself at the point of 1 to 5 and check at what scale you are at present and then plan to improve.

Assignment:

Q1: What do you prepare before going to the prospect: I prepare my checklist, my brochure. I check with customer for appointment.

Q 2: Problem questions Solution questions.

What you do after the meeting?

How you close the sale:

Feedabck and close the sales

MASTERING THE "GAME OF SELLING"

What product knowledge is not how much you know about your product but it is how you present the knowledge to the customer for his problem solution. You don't need to share the entire benefits in one go because average prospect only remembers one benefit. We thought we have to provide all the information to prove our product's success.

Sales Is all about positioning and its about YOU. The second secret is identifying the prospect.

1. They must have need for your product.
2. They must have the authority and ability to pay for your product.
3. They have the sense of urgency for the decision to buy the product.
4. Trust: People buy from whom they trust.
5. Willing to listen to you: They should be willing to listen to you.

CHAPTER 4

Prospecting: First Step for Sale Journey

MASTERING THE "GAME OF SELLING"

In today's world selling is not easy. You cannot wait for the customer to visit you. In this E-age, you need to go out and find out your prospects with the help of various tools. You have to be creative for searching the prospects. The first step for the sale is to have the right prospect in your hand. The first questions that come in our mind: How to get the prospect for our product? Where is my target audience and how I can approach them? Which are the methods available for finding the prospects?

Prospecting is the first step for sales. As a salesman, you need to keep your funnel full with lots of prospects. It is the lifeline for a salesman. Daily prospecting is required to keep the ball rolling. Sales professional always involved in so many activities like order closing, delivery tracking and machine installation and regular meeting with existing prospects and making sales presentation to every suspect and during this they forget the key of prospecting.

Target your segment and generate the leads: In the sales process, you first need to target your market segment. You need to analyse the potential of the segment. It is always better to work in the segment where you can achieve the success. Before selecting a segment you need to measure the gap of required product in that segment.

How can I target my focus segment: Like Glass, Ceramic, SWM and Construction?

The concern and pain areas of the prospects and how your product can bridge the gap: What are the concerns these industries are facing? Are they having the right product for their application? How my product can add values in these industries?

I would like to share a Shoe Salesman Story: This simple story is one that I've heard a few times now and it illustrates the above point really well. This story really taught about the salesman's attitude towards prospecting.

Two shoe salesmen were sent to Africa to see if there was a market for their product.

The first salesman visited Africa, visited the market and checks the shoe requirement. After the study he reported back, *'This is a terrible business opportunity, no-one wears shoes. Please book my return tickets to India. There is no point wasting time and money in this market.'*

After few months, the company again decides to send the second salesman. The second salesman reached Africa, visited the market and said what a market, great potential and reported back, *"This is a fantastic business opportunity, no-one wears shoes."*

Please extend my stay, send me few more shoe samples and we have great opportunity here.

The only question that I have is, when confronted with a problem or challenge, which salesman are you?

How to target your customer

After selecting and zeroing down on the segment, the next step is how to target the customer.

Targeting is required before moving into sales field. You are not going to sell your product to the entire world in one go. You need to eat the elephant in pieces. You need to target your prospects, their buying power & their problem areas. I draw a pie chart and target my market. You need to analyse the total market. You need to target the right customer,

Potential Customers

What are the filters you use to target your market?

1. Company Size: Their production and daily usage
2. Location: Where the company is situated
3. Segment: In which segment they are dealing
4. Current equipment: Which current equipment they are using

Brian Tracy says:

> Keep your sales pipeline full by prospecting continuously.
> Always have more people to see
> than you have time to see them.
>
> -Brian Tracy

Who is Prospect and Suspect?

You need to identify that who is the prospect of your product and who is suspect for you?

Every lead you are getting from your funnel needs to analyse between suspect vs prospect.

A suspect could be anyone, whereas a prospect is one who meets the following three criteria:

1) A need for your product
2) Ability to take decision
3) Money to buy your product

> If any one of above is missing, he is not your prospect…Keep your focus on your target segment. Beware that you cannot sell warm clothes in summer season…To maintain a constant flow of prospects in your funnel one needs to have multiple channels. The salesperson over a period of time will develop his own level of comfort in the prospecting method.

Sources of New Prospects: To generate new prospects, one can do the following activities:

1. **Same industries where you got success:** The best way to start prospecting is to look for the industries or segments where your product has proven its value. You can search for the database of same segment through various channels. You can ask for the list of industries from your existing customers. You can do the segmentation and prepare a list of all the available prospects in A Class, B Class and C class categories.

2. **Referrals from existing customers:** The best way to promote your product is to get the referrals from existing customers. They know about all the related industries. They know who is actually looking for your product or where your product can be more successful. Be in touch with your customers; keep them happy and satisfied with the product. Provide them good services and response. Ask from your customers regarding the same type of industries and the way they are doing their job. Ask from them the references in their friend group. You can easily sell the products to references. If you have a good relationship with your existing customers, you can easily get the repeat orders and you can provide their reference if someone needs feedback from existing customers.
3. **Industry association meets:** Another good opportunity you can grab is by promoting your product in various association meets. All same type of industries organise their association meetings and come out with their directory annually. You must keep an eye on all such types of event to directly communicate with target audience at such platforms.
4. **Cold calling to customers:** This is one of the oldest and best methods to find out the right prospect. You must have habit of cold calling to prospects. You must make a target of 101 calls in a week as per your industry. You can be very successful in sales if you win over cold calling technique. During cold calls, be very polite and ask for the permission to explain about your product or ask for the right person to contact.
5. **Advertisement:** Advertisement at the right place also provides good results. You can promote

your product with an advertisement in the local newspaper, magazines and industry directory.

6. **Customer meet**: Customer meet is also a good technique to generate prospects. You can select a location near to your target segment and can call 30-40 prospects for the meet. You can convey your product presentation and get a chance to interact with all competition customers and prospects at one place. It is an experience that in every customer meet you can easily get one to two prospects who can buy your product. Customer meets are a low-cost affair and you can choose the location and food as per your marketing budget.

7. **Demonstration:** In case of new products, people buy the product after seeing and real-time experience. Demonstration plays a very important role for the confidence building in the prospect's mind. You can demonstrate, at the prospect site, the application of your product and showcase the advantage of your product. With the demonstration at customer site, the customer can easily see the benefits of the products in terms of cost saving and automation in his regular working, he can also calculate the ROI of the product and can measure the productivity with respect to his existing equipments. The demonstration plays a role in tangible products while in the case of intangible products customer testimonials will play the major role.

8. **Awareness campaign:** You can start the awareness campaign about your product and services. When people will get the knowhow about your product and services they will start approaching you for the same. The awareness campaign can be done with any marketing agency and/or by setting up a small canopy in the targeted area.

9. **Competition customers:** The best way to generate the prospect is by visiting the competition customers. You can easily get the database of the customers using the competition products. You can visit them and can get the information about the experience with their existing product, the concerns and issues they are facing with the product and you can offer them your product with the better feature and support system. People are always open for better option and service system.
10. **Telemarketing:** You can always generate the business with telemarketing. The marketing agencies can contact with the prospect and can promote your products among the customers. Then, you can contact the interested prospects.
11. **Hiring of consultants to find out prospects:** For generating new prospects, you can hire available consultants in the market. Some time they have access to all the target audience and customers. They can do the telemarketing for you to find out the prospects. They can also work for the target segments and can provide you prospects' list based on category.
12. **Trade shows and events:** Trade shows and events provide good opportunity to show case your product to mass market. You must showcase your products or services for the product awareness for prospect generation.
13. **Online marketing:** Online marketing of products also generate good no. of prospects these days. People are using goggle and search engines to find out the required products. Your presence on World Wide Web plays major role. You can promote on Facebook, Twitter and Instagram. Nowadays, people compare the available products online before taking the final decision.

14. **Networking:** Networking with the people in the same field or industries always provide the clue to the prospect. Networking with financiers and banking institutions can provide you the list who are looking for such products. The networking with other industries who also supply or provide technical knowhow can provide you the prospects.
15. **Factory visit/Site visit:** To generate the confidence in the prospects' mind, one needs to take the prospect to factory/site. It always build confidence in the prospect's mind.
16. **The Prospect Funnel:** In prospecting, the prospect funnel is important. The hooper of the funnel should always be full with prospects. As per the below mentioned funnel, it is very clear that if you got 48 prospects then you will be able to get 24 appointments and after meeting with 24 prospects you will find out approximately 12 A class prospects for your product. After submitting the quotes and follow-ups, you will be able to close 4 sales.

Octopus Principle for Segment Planning: One needs to plan for the targeted segments based on the octopus figure. As an octopus is having various hands, a salesman should focus on various target segments. The target segments/markets will give you base to grow.

The salesman should have prospecting attitude. Prospecting is an art and the lifeline for sales. Prospecting is a continuous process which should be done on a daily basis. Without regular prospecting, the sale funnel will start depleting.

During prospecting, the salesman should have an eagle eye. He should keep his eyes and ears open to find out the prospects in the market.

The best way of prospecting is to regularly visit the industries where you have gained success. It is always easy to expand horizontally in the same type of industries to replicate the product success.

For the prospecting, you can network with the sales people of other industries and within your own organisation.

The utmost important part is that always handle your prospect with care.

Prospect Sheet

It is very important to create a prospect sheet for regular followups and track records for your prospects. The below mentioned prospect sheet is very handy to manage your prospects.

S.No	Prospect Name	Address and Mobile No.	Category	Product Required	Remarks
1	XYZ	ABC	A	SSL	Will close the product in March 2017

You just need to enter prospect name, their contact details and mention the category like A Class, B Class or C Class. A class prospects are those which can be closed in 30-45 days, B class prospects are those which can be closed in 45-90 days and C class prospects are those which take more than 90 days to make decision. You have to keep records of all your prospects in your prospects database.

Prospect Sheet					
S.No.	Customer Name	Location	Configuration or Description	Category A/B/C	Remarks

My Cold Calling Sheet:

Your Mobile Calling Scorecard
Name: Date:
Prospecting Record:
Monday   1 2 3 4   5 6 7 8 9 10
Tuesday   1 2 3 4   5 6 7 8 9 10
Wednesday   1 2 3 4   5 6 7 8 9 10
Thursday   1 2 3 4   5 6 7 8 9 10
Friday   1 2 3 4   5 6 7 8 9 10
Saturday   1 2 3 4   5 6 7 8 9 10
1 2 3 4   5 6 7 8 9 10
Total Dials:
Total Appointments Schedule
Positive Leads
My Appointment for the Week
My Follow Up Calling

Demo Plan							
S.No	Zone	Segment	Customer Name	Location	Start date	Duration	Remarks

CHAPTER 5

Negotiation: The Key for Closing the Sale

MASTERING THE "GAME OF SELLING"

It is a fundamental skill that we need to learn on how to use the negotiation techniques for closing the sale. It is a scientific and conceptual framework.

Negotiation is general human behaviour, every customer before making a final purchase ask for better price and services. Negotiation is an important milestone which needs to be crossed with care to get the final order from the customer. It should be a win-win situation for both the buyer and seller.

Everyone negotiates every day, often without even considering it as a negotiation. The study of subject is called negotiation theory. Negotiation theorists differentiate the negotiation in two ways. First is Distributive Negotiation and the second is Integrative Negotiation.

Integrative Negotiation is also called interest-based, merit-based or principle-based negotiation.

Distributive negotiation is also sometimes called positional or hard bargaining negotiation. It's tends to approach negotiation on the model of haggling.

In every deal, before closing the sale and getting the purchase order from customer, the important phase of negotiation starts. The customer tries to get the best price with his negotiation ability. During this process of so-called negotiation, the customer starts his attempt to negotiate and we need to understand Negotiation vs Haggling.

Negotiation is a discussion & dialogue between two parties aimed at reaching an agreement and trying to arrive at a Win-Win situation.

Haggling is bargaining persistently, especially over the cost of something, where both parties feel they lose……

For example, in my recent visit to one of the customer sites for closing the deal, the customer started the negotiation process with Sales engineer. The customer asks, what better you can do, the Sales engineer says, 'That is the best I can do? They both initiate the negotiation…The Customer starts by either reducing the price or asking for consumable parts as free of cost or free extended warranty etc…'

The customer haggles and gets some more…The sales engineer haggle and gives in a little more and eventually they strike a bargain somewhere …after they have signed the Purchase order (PO) and delivers the Loadall to customer. The customer feels that he could have squeezed the seller little more and seller feels he gave away too much.

Let's understand the flow:

Customer: We are interested in your Telehandler …What is your Price?

Sales Engineer: Sir, The Basic Price is Rs 24.5 Lakh plus Taxes….

Customer: That's your quoted price? Give me your better price (He has not made any counter offer.)

Sales Engineer: Sir…We can give you Rs 50,000 as cash discount and Rs 30,000 additional FOC.

Customer: I am comparing it with other Tractor Loaders. They are available at low cost…Give me your best price.

MASTERING THE "GAME OF SELLING"

Sales Engineer: He builds on versatility part of the Loadall.... and Increase FOC to Rs 50000...

Customer: Give me your last Price ....I will discuss with my partner's....

Sales Engineer: He further increases the cash discount to Rs 75000...

Before any counter offer of Customer, the sales engineer offered Rs 75000 as a cash discount and 50K as an FOC.

This is called haggling and peddling. This is not negotiation and selling. The seller knows that haggling is a way of life and the customer knows that if he doesn't haggle, he will be cheated. If this is the way you do business then you need to relook the process.

We also need to understand the types of negotiators.

a) Soft bargainers: These people see negotiation as too close to competition, so they choose a gentle style of bargaining.

b) Hard bargainers: These people use contentious strategies to influence, utilising phrases as "this is my final offer" and "take it or leave it".

c) Principled bargainers: Individuals who bargain this way seek integrative solutions and do so by sidestepping commitment to specific positions.

A good negotiation is a process in which we need to understand the following. It involves three basic elements: **process, behaviour and substance.**

1) Mutual respect with preparation and planning: You need to respect customer point of view and understand him. You need to approach him with your complete preparation and planning. Everyone is different. Treat the customer how they want to be treated.
2) Handling Issues with clarification and justification: Handle customer issues one by one and provide solution. Never assume their problems. Ask more questions and decide in advance how to resolve the differences.
3) Stay focused on the discussions related to your product.
4) Accept responsibility with problem solving.
5) Understand customer expectation first and close the deal.
6) In negotiations, never assume a fixed pie.
7) Never underestimate your negotiation power and skills.

You need to plan your negotiation strategy with the customer. You need to use the key tactics during the negotiation stage with difficult customers.
We negotiate on daily basis with wife, with kids & with colleagues. Negotiation skills are very important in your career advancement.

Plan and Prepare your Negotiation Strategy: You need to decide whether your negotiation process is position-based or interest-based. Also decide whether this negotiation is for dispute resolution or deal making. Complete your negotiation analysis, including: setting a reservation price and stretch goal, identifying alternatives to a deal and finding the zone of potential agreement.

Use a decision tree to determine your BATNA (Best Alternative to a Negotiated agreement).

Resolve Ethical Issues in Negotiations: There is always a challenge to maintain your ethics. How to manage ethical issues, e.g., Law-based ethical standard: As per law, you need to drive right hand drive car. It is a law-based ethic.

Do you deliberately lie to prospect during negotiation? Always ensure that you have to be very clear in communication for providing the right information to the prospect, never lie about any information or over promise to get the order.

Negotiation Tactics: Use the key tactic during the discussion and get the purchase order. During negotiations, avoid the traps and close the deal to get the purchase order.

Assessing your Negotiation Style: Exercise for evaluating the negotiation style.
Instructions: Listed below are the important traits of a person's negotiating style and approach. Each trait demonstrates a wide range of variations. This can be organised along a continuum, as has been done below.

1 Goal: What is your goal in all business negotiations: a binding contract or creation of a relationship.

⟵—————————⟶

Contract   Relationship

2. Attitude:

Win/Lose   Win/Win

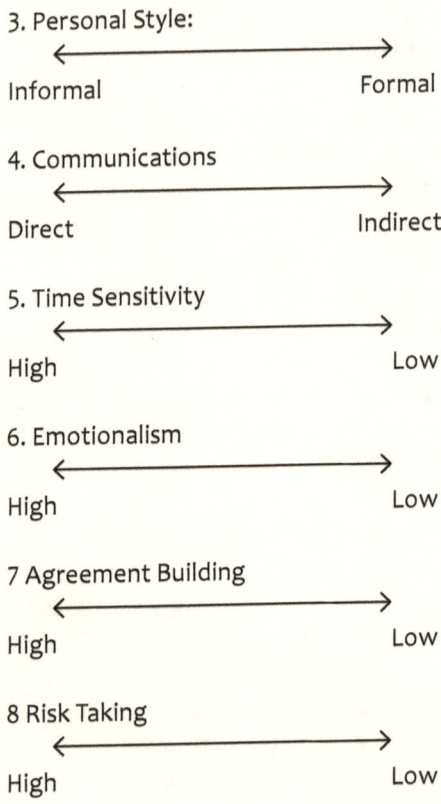

Analyse your negotiation process: Rate yourself on the basis of the above mentioned exercise. Successful negotiators always analyse their negotiation process.

Each has something to offer. Negotiation can also be collaborative efforts. In negotiation, both parties receive. There is a wide variety of negotiations; it's a very critical component.

It is important to understand that there are no rules for negotiations. Negotiation is not selling; it is the process to close the sales.

Gerard Nierenberg, who has been referred to as the father of negotiation by the Wall Street Journal says that whenever people exchange ideas with the intention of changing relationships, whenever they confer for agreement, then they are negotiating. Nierenberg's statement is further developed by Israel Unterman who said, negotiation is conducted neither to widen nor breach the relationship, but to form a new or different configuration.

CHAPTER 6

Closing the Sale with Closing Techniques

MASTERING THE "GAME OF SELLING"

'A sale is not something you pursue; it's what happens to you while you are immersed inserving your customer.' - Unknown

Closing the sale: The most important part in sale process is closing the sale and getting the Purchase order from the customer. A sales man find out the prospect, provide him the product information through presentation and demonstration of the product and last important point in his journey is to close the sale with the order from customer. Many times, a salesperson fails in the last part of the sale, they are not able to close the sale. Selling is not an easy job, it is really hard work.

Always before providing the purchase order, customer clarifies his objection and doubts. There is no sale happen without clarifying customer doubts. When customer start asking question related to product performance, delivery and pricing it clearly indicates that he is interested in your product. At that time it is sales person responsibility to clarify all doubts of the customer and get the order.

A successful salesman has good experience in objection handling. It is responsibility of the salesman to work on FAQ. Based on the field experience one can prepare about the frequently asked questions. The salesman should have point to point answers on the FAQ.

Customer Testimonials: It always provides a good impression on the customer if you have customer testimonials. Always ask for the testimonials from a happy customer. The customer testimonial is really a good selling tool.

Product Costing: The major objection before closing the deal is regarding pricing. Customer will always say that your pricing is high. You should provide proper justification about the pricing of the product with respect to product quality and value it provides to customer in terms of productivity, quality and safety. If the product pricing is justifiable, every customer will be ready to provide you the order.

Listening to Customer requirement: Always listen to customer requirement and problem with empathy & respect. Most of the times, a salesman is aware about the customer concern, and that he needs to keep his patience and listen to customer and take a pause before replying. He should complement to the customer for raising his point. It gives feeling to customer that he is listened properly. Then provide to the point answers for his concern and build the confidence about the product.

Customer Problem Solution: Always provide solution to customer, it will create the requirement of your product.

Answers to Customer Question: Reply the answer to customer queries to satisfy the customer issues and objections.

Answers to Product Issues: If customer ask for any product issue, then you should be ready with the improvements done in the product and ensure the customer about the reliability of the product.

Closing Techniques: In sales, the most important part is to ask for the order from the prospect. Studies show that salesperson fears in asking the order due to the fear of rejection. If you have presented well then simply ask for the order and close the sale. I am sharing below mentioned sales closing techniques which will be very useful for closing the sale.

1. **Ben Franklin Sale closing technique:** Mr. Ben Franklin was born in Philadelphia in 1975. He was a very famous American statesman.
   This technique is also called as Balance Sheet closing technique. In this technique, the salesperson and customer jointly work on pros and cons sheet. The salesperson helps in building the cons sheet and the prospect registers his pros for the same. In the end, the sheet is helpful for the customer to decide about the product.

2. **The Alternative Option close:** In this technique, the salesman offer the alternative to the customer in terms of colour or variant. This technique is also known as positive choice close.
3. **Direct order:** In this technique, the salesperson directly asks for the order from the prospect. The salesman should use this technique only when he is fully confident that the customer has made up his mind and is ready for the placement of the order.
4. **Assumptive close:** In this closing technique, the salesperson assumes that the buyer has decided for the product and he asks for the purchase order and the system of billing from the customer. In this technique, the salesman explain the next step for buying of the product.
5. **Sale by product demo:** This sale process is like Puppy Dog sales technique. In this sale process, the salesman and the company provides the product to the customer for demo and use for few days. After the demonstration and use, it builds confidence in the customer's mind or he gets used to it for the process. After the experience period, the salesman can ask for the order from the prospects. This technique is very proven technique worldwide for the orders. This technique is developed as the name

suggests that one salesman used to provide the puppy to the prospect for the feeling of the puppy at home for weekend. After the experience most of the prospects are ready to buy the puppy.

6. **The Purchase Order Close:** In this technique, the salesperson after the complete presentation and discussion takes out the purchase order form and fill out the customer details with the product required by the customer with other commitments he has made with the prospect while closing the same. This is a very fast and effective way of closing the sale.

7. **Success Story Close:** The success story close is most powerful closing technique. It provides confidence to the prospect about the success of product in similar applications. The salesman can share the product success stories of the same segment to close the deal. He can share that how the other same segment company was facing the concern and after successful installation of equipment or machinery they are very happy with the productivity & manpower saving. At this stage, I would like to share a success story from my own sales experience: I was meeting with a new prospect at Morbi Gujarat. In the Silicate manufacturing industries they need to handle glass for feeding to hot burners. They used to do the same job with manpower and facing major concern with safety and non-availability of manpower at required time. They installed our material handling equipment and realised that the equipment is very useful for such glass handling application. I provided the same reference and success story to all similar industries and got good orders from the same segment.

8. **Face-to-face Close:** Most of the customers would like to close the order during face-to-face meetings.

You need to fix up the appointment and meet them for the order closing.

9. **Senior Close:** Most of the prospect close the case with your senior. You take the prospect till the verge of customer and call the senior. Such customer always would like to close the case after discussion with your senior. It provide confidence to customer that he met with senior person of the company and got the right product at right price.

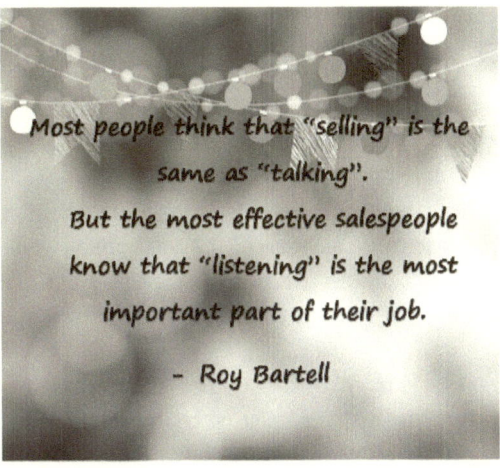

> Most people think that "selling" is the same as "talking".
> But the most effective salespeople know that "listening" is the most important part of their job.
>
> - Roy Bartell

10. **Objection handling:** For closing the sale, the objection handling plays a very important role. You should prepare yourself about the common objections raised by the prospects for your product.

Closing on Pricing or Solution: You need to plan in advance that you are going to close the sale on pricing or solution provided by your product.

Action Plan:

1) Note down which closing technique work for you and why?

2) Analyse your sale closing process & write down the learning.

Reference Selling

I believe that reference selling is very important part of selling process. You can also call it a relationship selling. You contact the prospect based on the reference provided by your existing customer or your friend or relative, etc.

The repeat sales from the existing customers and the selling from the references from existing customers is required for the development for business. The word of mouth publicity and references creates a good percentage of business. The best salesperson makes it a habit to get the reference from existing customers and prospects. They make all-time high sales with referrals. The referral is more valuable and worth is very high as compared to cold calling. Referral selling is one of the fastest way to increase sale and income. When you are visiting someone on referral the chances of closing the sale is very high. You are approaching the right target audience based on someone's reference and you will get the automatic credibility of the person who has given the reference. You need to build good relationship with your existing clients so that you can ask for reference every time you meet with them.

When you get a referral you need to act fast. Call the person that you got the reference from so and so and you would like to meet with them regarding the product which is running successfully on your friend site.

Thanks note: Always write a note of thanks for the person who has provided the referral after closing the sale.

Always Leverage your reference: Whenever you meet with any prospect or client ask for reference. For example, you visited an existing customer on a courtesy call and while leaving his office you asked for the reference and he provided you with two or three references then your prospect funnel will always be filled with A class prospects. Your happy customers are your core referral. Always make visits to your core referrals and thank them for every success on sales you achieved through their reference.

Act on your Referrals: Always take care of your referral base and try to increase your referral base. Build your referral base by building long-term relationship with your customers. Support them when they ask for any services in urgency. Deposit more in relationship and it will pay back to you in terms of more sales.

> IN THE SALES PROFESSION,
> THE REAL WORK BEGINS
> AFTER THE SALE IS MADE
> *-Brian Tracy*

> If you are not taking care of
> your customer,
> your competitor will.
> -Bob Hodey

CHAPTER 7

Goal Setting

'You see things; and you say, Why?" But I dream things that never were; and I say – Why not?'

- George Bernard Shaw

Goal setting is very important for every Individual. You must write down your professional and personal goals. If you want to grow in your life then start writing your goals. You are the CEO of your life, of your own Incorporation. If a company can have Vision and Mission and targets for growth then why we as individuals are not planning the Vision and Mission of our lives.

'The things that get scheduled are the things that get done.'

The Goals should be SMART:

Specific: Always plan specific goals.

Measurable: The goals should be measurable.

Achievable: The goals should be achievable and keep you motivated to achieve it.

Realistic: Always plan for realistic goal.

Time Bound: The goal should be time-bound. Always plan for short-term and long-term goals.

For Goal Setting exercise, you need to plan the Personal, Mental, Physical, Family, Financial & Spiritual goals.

> **Brian Tracy: Goals in Writing**
>
> 'Goals in writing are dreams with deadlines.'
>
> – *Brian Tracy*

Your **Personal Goals** are your own goals for your career and growth in life. Plan short-term and long-term goals for yourself.

Mental Goals: Your mental goals are your educational goals. Always be learning. When you stop learning then your growth curve will start to decline.

Physical Goals: Your physical goals are your Health Goals. A healthy man can only achieve his goals and can work for his passion. Somebody has well said that 'Health is Wealth'.

Family Goals: Family is the important part of your life journey. Nothing is permanent in life but your family will stay with you in phase of your life. Always plan for family.

Financial Goals: Finance is the driver of the life. You must plan for your financial goals wisely. Early start is the key to wealth generation.

Spiritual Goals: For Peaceful and happy life start planning your spiritual goals. Start mediation for keep your mind in peace. Start visiting to spiritual places as per your spiritual goal in life.

MASTERING THE "GAME OF SELLING"

Goals	Short-Term	Long-Term
Personal Goals		
Mental Goals		
Physical Goals		
Family Goals		
Financial Goals		
Spiritual Goals		

> 'Success is not measured by how high we go up in life, but how many times we bounce back after we fall down.'

I would like to share a Goal setting story with you. Everyone would like to achieve big in life, they have dreams and desires.

A study has been conducted at Harvard University. One of the researchers conducted a study with the graduating batch of 1953. This was the class of excellent students from one of the best institutes in the world. During the study, he observed that how many elite class students have clearly written specific goals and plans for next 20 years. One can consider that all of these must be having their goals for future. Surprising facts came out in the research that only 3% of the students were having the specific written goals. After 20 years, the same researcher studied the same batch of students to find out how they are doing in their life. During the study, it came out that only 3% who had clearly written goals are extremely successful and wealthy in their lives. They have accumulated the wealth, career and success they planned for themselves. The remaining 97% of the students were having average lifestyle, their combined wealth was less than the above 3% who had achieved as per their written goals.

I was also surprised with the story that how one can achieve more if he is having written goals and other is just thinking about his goals. The written goals are like blueprint. I thought of putting the same experiment on myself. I wrote goals for my personal development and professional growth. To my surprise, all goals converted into reality with time. One day, I took my goal setting sheet and it gives me a big surprise that some power has provided me all what I have written on the paper to achieve in my life.

> 'Setting Goals is the first step in turning the invisible into visible.' – Tony Robbins

Let's Plan for Goal Setting: Suppose your doctor just declared that you have only one year in your life? What would you like to achieve in this one year. Write your goal today and make an action plan to achieve them. Action without plan is time waste and you will not achieve anything in life. An organised plan of action is required to achieve goals. You can accomplish your goals in one year if you have written goals.

Focus: The Sales executive should have focus on his target. In this economic scenario, you can use your potential to earn and grow in the field of sales.
Your Priority, focus and concentration is the key to success. These are the characteristics that can be developed and used by all successful people in their daily life. You need to unleash your power.

The power of clarity: you must have clarity of your goals. The clearer you are with your goals the fast you will achieve your goals. Clear goals will provide you the way and motivation to achieve them.
Since ages, the story of Eklavya (a character from the Indian epic- Mahabharata) has come to define exemplary discipleship. But there is an unheard and unseen side to the famous story.

Eklavya was the son of poor hunter. He wanted to learn the art of archery to save the deer in the jungles and protect his family from the attack of animals. He visited Dronacharya to learn the art of archery, Dronacharya as teacher of prince is not allowed to teach anyone from outside the royal family. He denied to Eklavya for his teachings, but Eklavya accepted him as a guru in his mind. He went to his home and made a statue of his guru and started learning the archery in the presence of statue. By his day and night practice and sincerity he learnt the art of archery. One day Arjuna heard that someone in the jungle is very famous archrer, he visited the jungle and observed that Eklavya is very talented then he asked from him, who taught you archery. Eklavya hints towards the statue of Dronacharya. By seeing the Dronacharya statue Arjuna got annoyed and asked from the Dronacharya why he is teaching someone out of Royal family. Dronacharya Surprised and visited the site and met with Eklavya, to his surprise he found that Eklavya a very talented and skilled archiest. Eklavya welcomed his teacher wholeheartedly and show his talent to his teacher and shared that he learnt all in presence of his statue. Dronacharya asked for Guru Dakshina (Guru Dakshina is like a fee student pays to his teacher at the end of the course). Eklavya as a devotee and student of Drnacharya agrees for the same and committed to his guru for the Guru Dakshina. At that moment Guru Dronacharya asked for his right thumb as a guru dakshina. The Eklavya immediately take out the knife and cut his thumb and presented to guru as a dakshina.

We observed that in this story Dronacharya seems to be selfish and done injustice to Eklavya. But Dronacharya uplifted the Eklavya from a student to epitome of discipleship. The universe still remembers the Eklavya as an example of Guru Shishya parampara. (Student & Teacher relationship). When people think of respecting guru and devotion they always remember Eklavya. In this story the Dronacharya took the entire blame on himself and uplifted Eklavya an example.

MASTERING THE "GAME OF SELLING"

The power of focus: You know what you want to achieve. Goal setting process is simple and powerful

Decide exactly what you want: write down what you want in your life. Forget about past and limitation.

Be specific: be specific what you want in life.

If you ask people are they having goals? If you ask about their goals. They will say they want more money, car, big house, etc., these are wishes.

Only 3% of the people have set goals.

Write you goals. Make them specific and measurable.

When you write down your goals it will move you in top 3 percent of the people.

Set the deadlines to achieve your goals. The law of attraction will start working for you.

Set deadline for weekly, monthly and yearly goals. Some time you will achieve your goals before timeline.

Identify the additional skills and resources you require to achieve your goals. Always divide your goals in small activities, in sequence with priority. You cannot eat the elephant in one go, divide it into small pieces.

Use 80/20 rule. 20% of activities will help you to achieve 80% of the results.

Einstein says nothing happen if you will not take the first step.

Take action: Take action to achieve your goals.

Your self-confidence will increase if you take the first step. Well begin is half done. Write down your ten goals you want to achieve in your life

What is your no. 1 most important goal in your life.

What action you will take every day to achieve this goal. What qualification and people you need to achieve this goal. This is your definite purpose. The single goal will provide you focus and clarity in your life to achieve the goal.

The power of purpose: what is the purpose of your life? The two days are important in your life the day you born and the day you will leave this earth. Each person is design to fit in somewhere. People have two types of needs.

Write you mission statement: You have seen that companies have their mission and vision statement. As a person, you should have your own personal mission and vision statement.

Your mission statement: What is the main purpose of your life? The mission statement can include what you want to be in life, your values and mission of life.

You need not to compromise in your life. Stick to the values. How your values practiced in your life.

Vision: you should have clear vision for yourself. You should be clear. Make your vision a reality.

What is your mission and vision in life: most company spends great time to set up their mission and vision statement. As a human being you should be very clear about your mission and vision statement. Write down the method to achieve your mission.

Our mission is to provide our customer the best product and services.

As a person you must create your mission in life and your vision.

Mission can be accomplished.

Mission: Your mission is important, you are so important in your life, you need a personal mission statement. There is a ripple effect, what you do in life it will multiply and get back to you with its impact. It's your duty to bring value to this universe.

My mission Statement: My mission is to educate and empower sales people to achieve their sales target and personal goal in life.

I Am Important: You need to realise that you are important for this universe. You are on earth to play an important role. You are here for a purpose. Everything on earth has a purpose. Look at the miracle of nature, nature turns a seed into a tree.

You have two types of Purpose:

1 Purpose of Life: What's the purpose of your life? Your need to identify your life purpose. There are three important elements of life.

1. Add Value: You need to add value to the world. You are so important that you are adding value to the world.
2. Learn & Grow: To evolve mentally, emotionally and spiritually you need to learn and grow.

3. Enjoy: To enjoy this journey, you have one lifetime so enjoy the life.

To determine your mission, if you have all the money you want to spend what you will choose to do and what you will love to do.

What type of difference you want to create in the world?

A desire of feeling important creates the difference. Take some time to write down your mission statement.
My mission is to educate and empower sales people to achieve their sales target and personal goal in life.

Vision

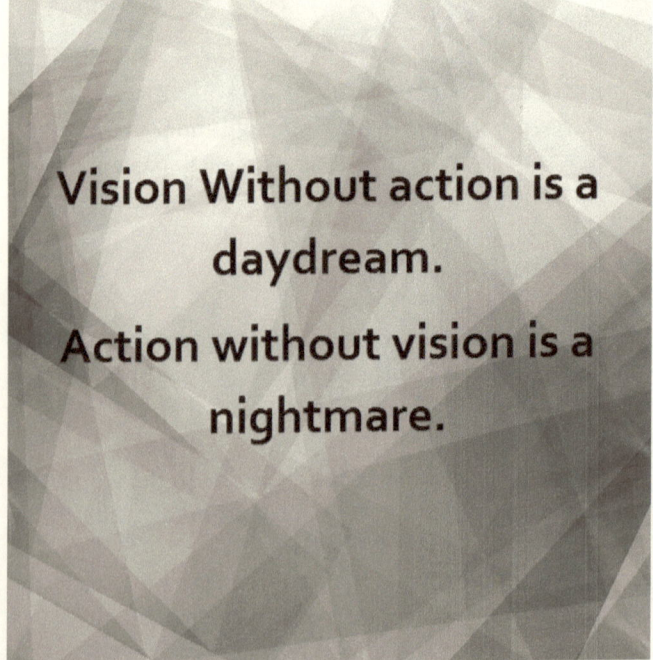

Vision is a snapshot of an ideal way to see yourself in business or career. Your vision must be ignite you. You must be willing to give up your life fully for your vision.

Miracle happens when your passion meets with commitment.

Passion + commitment = Miracle

Create a Vision Board for your dream and Goals. Your vision board should have all your wild ideas and goals for your life.

Whatever you want to achieve in life start writing on your vision board with images and pictures.

Paste the images with timeline to achieve. The vision board will be converted into the reality. Your subconscious mind will start believing it and the law of attraction will bring out opportunities to convert that vision into reality.

Vision Board

Clarity: 'Clarity is lack of obstacle.' Clarity is a natural state. It comes from removing the blocks. Why you are here on this earth?

Whats the Purpose: Everyone on earth has a purpose.

Invisible ------------Visible

Secret of Life: 'The secret of life is Know Thyself.' You are on earth to perform your duty.

There is a specific law of Dharma = Duty

You have a secret contract with divinity. Each person has a specific calling. You are important and unique.

The power of concentration: You can achieve your goals when you have concentration. Everything is hard before it becomes easy, We are what we repeatedly do. Practice makes permanent.

Addicted to distraction: Phone, Facebook, etc., are creating the distractions to your way to success. We are continuously checking messages and mails. You start your day with checking WhatsApp...You are now addicted to it.

Results: The most important measurable parameter is the results. Results are required in smart goals. Specific, measurable, realistic, achievable and time-bound goals. Personal management process.

1) Become absolutely clear about goals. Write goal for each area of your life. Set them as per your priority list. Finish what you start. Practice and prepare a checklist to measure the progress.

Make a list of task you want to accomplish. Best time to prepare a list is night before you want to start next day. List the task you want to complete in this week or on the day. A list is sequence to control your day. It will set priority before you start your work: Sometime, it is 80-20 rule or 90-10 rule. 20% of the items will generate 80% of the results.

Most people procrastinate and delay the work. Work extends as the time available. Procrastinating about the success and work, Categories them as ABC type of category to your work focus on your A task. The A, B & C types are the work based on the priority. Spend your time for A task, eliminate the tasks which are not required. Start doing things which are important for you.

Social networking is social no working. Just say no to the activity which is of no value and time waster.

How to set priorities. What is the most valuable use of my time?

Set priorities: what work I do & which will create the difference in my life. Your ability to choose one task will impact on your life.

In life, there is no appreciation of partial work completion. You need to complete the work you have started.

The power of excellence: You need to be an excellent personality what you do. Like yourself, the more you like yourself the more you like other people. it will create better immune system for you. The more you like yourself the better you perform, the better you get the better you will do the better you will perform.

The top 20% of the sale person earns 80% of the money. I was not good as door to door sales man. Everyone starts from the bottom. It is the secret that the top 20% today started from the bottom 20%. T Harv Eker once said every master once was a disaster.

3% vs 99%. The 3% of the people are having written clear goals. The 3% are achieving more than the remaining 97%. By writing your goals, you determine the amount you earn in your life.

Income gap vs skill gap: The people who continue to grow are those who believe in continual learning. They always learn new things, listen to audio books. We know the principal of compounding. You need to invest in yourself based on the same principle. What is the one excellent skill you have that is most helpful for your career.

What is your major definite purpose? Each person has some role to play. People have two type of needs. 98% of the people don't realise their full potential in their lifetime. What one thing you want to achieve and crate your legacy for the next generation.

Developing skills: Each skill you learn will increase your earning ability.

Keep learning: always keep learning. Always learn one new skill that help you to grow professional and at personal level. Make a list of the skills you want to learn and make the action plan. You have to be lifelong learner.

Continuous improvement: Learn new skills as your career is dependent on it. All skills are learnable. You are one skill away to double your productivity and income.

The power of people: The quality of your relationship decide the quantity of your relationship.

Make the list of all people you need in your life to achieve your goals. Make a list of your colleagues, bosses and mentor.

What is in it for my customer (WIIFMC): what's in it for my customer? You must become a go giver rather than go getter. Put in before you take out. The first type of person are: What can I get from this person. Network with many different people in society. The top 20% people don't waste their time on TV they spend their time to network people. Think from the top people, how they think. They think what I can give to this person. What is the most productive thing you can do to network with most successful people are doing. The top 20% people are always network with successful people.

One call away: You are just one call away to change your life, you never know who in your network is helpful for your growth at that moment. Keep expanding your network. Instead what they can do for you think what you can do for them. Write or mail a good article and send to the person who may like.

The success principle: The more you give the more will come back to you. When you expect something from that person you will not see that person again. You reap what you will sow as we know the law of nature.

Seven great behaviours: Make people feel important; Every person you meet make them feel important. Never criticise, condemn and misbehave with people. If you cannot speak nice it's better to be silent. Most people conversations start with negative. Don't join negative people and in their gossip behaviour.

Be agreeable: Be agreeable with people, people may ask to understand your position. In most cases be agreeable, Be cheerful & positive.

Practice acceptance: accept the person as they are, help them to increase their self-esteem. Just smile and accept the others as they are, add value and help them to increase their self-esteem. You improve your self-image if you start accepting others people as they are.

Appreciation: Say thank you and appreciate the people whom you meet. Appreciate for the best they have. They will remember you always. Appreciate them for the large and small things they do. When you thank a person they think good about themselves and good about you.

Admiration: Admire others and give them compliments, congratulate them for their achievement. Look for things and compliment them often. Compliment for their accomplishments. They like you more if you give compliments.

Express approval: You need to feel valuable. When you praise them their self-esteem will go up. Praise people when they are productive and helpful. Praise your kids and parents for their support and the things they do for you.

Give attention: Listen to people, give attention while they talk. Imagine that your eyes are sunlight, give other people the required sunlight.

Effective listening, pause before replying: The more you ask questions and listen to them the more the other person trusts you. Always ask Questions for clarification. There should not be any possibility for misunderstandings.

Feedback: This the real passive test. Ask for the feedback.

The key is to form good habit. Practice makes you perfect, it becomes permanent.

Power of excellence: The basic principal is self-esteem, like yourself; the more you like yourself the more you like other people. The more you like yourself, the productive and energetic you will become.

Power of persistence: Once you set the goal for yourself, your life will go in different directions. Set the big goals. One of my friend set the goal of double his income. Neapolitan hill said persistence is the character of man. There is no such thing as failure.

Character development: Stay calm and take a deep breath and relax. When you are in anger just relax and meditate. Stay calm

Get the facts: No situation as bad as it appears. Ask questions and check who is involved. Remain calm and take the control of thinking

Look good in every situation. When you look back in your life you can see there is always something good. Difficulty comes not to obstruct but to instruct. What is the biggest problem in your life today? Everyone is having the problems in their life. Look for the gift. The bigger the problem the bigger the gift is. Accept responsibility of the problem...say I am responsible for it. Each problem has solution...Focus on the solution.

Preprogrammed your mind. You respond in particular way when the problem arises. You never give up when the problem arises. In the case of adversity, you will automatically feel resilient. 50% problem can be solved very easily if you define them. What is the worst possible outcome of this problem?

Eliminate worry and stress: You have to eliminate worries and stress stored inside you.

CHAPTER 8

Sharpening the Saw

MASTERING THE "GAME OF SELLING"

> If I had six hours to chop down a tree, I'd spend the first four hours sharpening the axe. - Abraham Lincoln

Working on your life skills will help you achieve more in personal and professional life. One wiseman said that the best investment is investment on you.

When did you sharpen your Axe: We all heard about the story of a wood cutter, he was very hard working and engaged in tree cutting. On the very first day of his job, he cut 8 trees, on the next day he managed to cut only 5, though he worked very hard and completed 8 hours on his job. On the third day, he managed to cut only 3 trees, he felt very disappointed that why his performance was going down, he approached to his supervisor for the solution. The supervisor asked, 'Why don't you sharpen your saw?' The exhausted woodcutter replied that "I do not have the time to do all these things." I just need to cut the wood!

The same principle applies in our personal and professional life. We have to give inputs to our mind for better performance. The self-development is the best investment on the earth. Every day you need to give some time to yourself to sharpen your saw. Provide input to your mind and body by reading books related to your profession by attending seminars and courses.

I would like to share one real story. I organised one training session for my dealer team. One of the persons was not doing well in his sales profession and was very depressed by not getting any orders. After attending the training he bought one book on sales and decided to read it 20 min every day. In a month's time, a miracle happened and he started selling and performing well in his field. He started building good relationship with clients and prospects.

Someone well said that "Reading is to the mind as exercise is to the body". The more you read the sharper and more alert you become. When you read more in selling, you learn more new ideas to sell.

The average adult reads less than one book a year. Many sales people do not read at all in the field of selling. In fact as per survey 90% of sales books are bought by customers who are not in the sales profession. Recently in Mumbai, I met with top salespersons of big MNCs and during discussion on sales I was amazed that how many books on sales they have read and are reading at present times. They sound like sale libraries with full knowledge on the subject.

Become an updated Professional: By getting up at 6:00 am in the morning and reading for 30 minutes on sales, you will find yourself reading about two sales book per month. Do you think that it will have an effect on your performance? The fact is that when you will read on the sales, you will become a subject matter expert with the right knowledge, skills, ideas, strategies and techniques for more sales. Your sales career and success will be in top gear. You will get the required promotion and growth in your field. Your Income and status will be double and tripled very fast.

> 'If you are not continually learning and upgrading your skills, somewhere, someone else is, and when you meet that person, you will lose.' - Reed Buckley

Sometime sales people complain that they have no time for learning and reading due to sales target and travelling. I would like to suggest that you can utilise your travelling time into learning time, while travelling in car, bus train or plane utilise your time for reading or listening sales talk or books. The average sale person drives 20,000km per annum and spend about 800 hourson the roads. He can utilise this time for listening audio program and as per study conducted by "University of California" that you can get the knowledge equivalent of a full time university education each year just by listening audio programs as you drive place to place.

Follow the Champions: The top sales people around the world read and listen to audio programs on sales. They utilise every second to increase their knowledge on sales. They are highest paid sales people and believe that listening to sales program has helped them to achieve the highest position in their career. The great tragedy is that the average salesperson waste his time for listening music and radio channels. They miss the time for great opportunity available to professional salesperson. It is said that radio is "chewing gum for ears". For the salesperson, listening to the radio is the equivalent of an athlete's dieting on candy and soft drinks. The best salesperson don't even know if their radio works because they never turn them on.

Improve Daily: Kaizen on yourself: Kaizen is a very famous Japanese term. In all Japanese companies, Kaizen is the way of working. First, let's understand what Kaizen is: Kai means change and Zen means better. Kaizen means change for the better. In all Japanese companies, all manufacturing team members need to implement one improvement on the line every day. I realised that in Sales Kaizen can do wonder. If our sale team member do one improvement in his daily sales call. It may be dealing with prospect, handling objection or improvement in closing the sale. He can analyse his sale call and then think in which area he can improve and implement that change next time. He will realise that his sale closing will increase and he will be in the top earner category.

It is your responsibility to make the client like you.
If they like you they will listen.
If they will listen they will believe.
If they believe they will buy.
-Zig Ziglar

If people like you, they'll listen to you.
But if they trust you, they'll do business with you.
-Zig Ziglar

Lost Sale

'Top salespeople understand they must learn to feel comfortable doing the uncomfortable-Tim

After so much effort, if salesman lost the sale. Then it becomes very important to analyse the lost sale. Wining back the competition customer in future is important to increase your future business. It is most important part of analaysis.

> 'Opportunities are never lost; someone
> will take the ones you miss.'-

Why we lost the order? Is it due to pricing or quality issue? We have to keep an eye on the competition vs our product pricing. Price positioning is very important. The over pricing of the product leads to sale losses.

Are we losing the case due to no follow up after submitting the quote? How many times we followed up with the customer. Or we missed the customer after submitting the quote.

We were not able to build the right connect with the customer. Sometimes, the salesman visits the prospect and does not build the connect with the customer. Building the connect with the customer to get the share of his mind for future business is important.

A good relationship should be developed with the customer to get the business from him.

> 'Your most unhappy Customers are your greatest source of learning.' - Bill Gates

CHAPTER 9

Sales Meetings

> "A Sales Guy asked at his performance meeting;
>
> "Which is your best sales figure"
>
> He Replied, "My Upcoming month Sales Figure"
>
> So let Your goal be better than before.

The sales meetings are a part of the Sales Executive's life. The seniors do the monthly, quarterly or annual sales review meetings with the team. What's the normal perception of Sales Meetings? Are these meetings motivational, inspirational or just sales beating?

Meetings are useful. We spend a lot of time in meetings. Seventy percent meetings are just waste of time. Purpose of the meeting should be crystal clear. Meeting is the time investment.

Agenda of the meeting should be very clear: What do we want to achieve in the meeting?

Meetings sometimes goes off the track.

Rules for better results during the meetings are as follows:

Meeting Start Time: It is very important to start the meeting on time. People wait for the latecomers who will hamper the flow of the meeting.

Interruptions: Phone calls, emails & uninvited guests in the meeting. You have to discipline in phone answering during the meeting. If possible switch off the mobiles or keep them on silent mode.

One should be inspired after the sales meetings not feel rejected or dejected.

If the sales meetings are happening for just the sake of sales meeting, just sharing the routine slides or performance numbers, then these will be boring. The sales meeting should be challenging, motivating, and useful.

What makes an effective executive: Professor and Author Peter Drucker in his Harvard Business Review article explained about what makes an effective executive. As Drucker said that 'Making a meeting Productive takes good deal of self-discipline.'

We have realised 4 types of behaviour in sales meetings which are as follows:

Learner: These executives show up early. Ready with their note pads, they gain as much as possible during the sales meetings. They know they will be able to apply the best practices shared during the meeting.

Vacationer: These executives treat sales meeting as vacations. They are present in the meeting for the sake of attendance. These people are semi-engaged and casual in approach.

Hostage: They are in the meeting because they are called for meeting. They have very less interest in meetings. They participate in the meeting when they are forced to participate.

Terrorist: They have hostile attitude during the meeting. They try to distract the people in the meeting.

Check your executives. In which category do they belong?

Points to be taken care of during the sales meeting are the following:

Lots of sales people think that the sales meeting will be held just to review your performance and products. There will be nothing to learn in those meetings. Their expectations will be to learn how to sell, where to sell and how to get the leads. The leader plays an important role in the sales meeting. It should not be sales beating and sales leader criticise poor performance. The facilitator should be encouraging and keep the team motivatedmotivation hog of the team. He is like a captain of the game.

Objective of the Sales Meetings: The agenda and objective of the sales meeting should be clear. Sales is a tough field. The facilitator should encourage for open ideas and appreciate the achievers.

Sharing of Success Stories: During the sales meeting, it is very important to share the success stories of the sales in the new area, new territories and new applications. It will be easy to replicate the success with horizontal deployment of same success in same industries within different territories.

Recognition to Achievers: It is required to recognise the achievers in each sales meeting. Everyone is looking for appreciation on front of large group. This boost person morale and confidence and drive towards bigger growth.

Co-ordination with Other Departments: The sales meeting should provide the platform for co-ordination and relationship building with other departments of the organisation. This indicates the relationship with service team, marketing team and new product development to focus on issues with priority.

Training and Way Forward: Each sales meeting should have training and experience sharing from company seniors. The sales executive should get the insight for business development.

Agenda for the Sales Meeting:

I am sharing the agenda for your reference. You need to set the agenda in advance so that people come prepared and feel motivated for the meeting.

Opening: The opening should be energetic with the recognition and sharing of success stories. In the opening meeting, one should share the achievement of top sales executive. The sales executive can share their learnings with the group. It will make the meeting interactive and live. It involves participation from everyone.

Training: In each meeting, ensure that after the opening session and sharing of success stories you keep the time for peer-to-peer training. Everyone has some positives and forte in sales.

Target Plan vs Actual: After the training, the facilitator should share the target vs actual status.

Before ending any meeting, only few meetings produce results.

Meeting and impact: Always review your meeting and analyse what impact your meeting has created. In meetings, assign the commitment with deadline and jot down the action plan and provide due acknowledgement and credit to the people.

In the meeting, the idea should be discussed in detail with big picture in the team members' mind.

In meetings, few personalities play important roles. These are as follows:

Explorers: They explore everything in detail about the target or idea.

Expert: These are experts and provide their expert comments.

Planner: They are good in planning and provide their inputs for action plan.

Energiser: They are full of energy and provide the required energy in the meeting. They are always helpful in creating the action plan.

Coach: Few act as a coach in the meeting with directions and guidelines.

One-to-one meeting: For effective outcome one-to-one meeting is useful. You focus on one target and strength. For better results, one-to-one meeting is recommended.

During the meeting you must pay attention and form an authentic connection with the team members. Always create positivity and Focus on strength of the individuals and the team.

In the meetings, ask for objectives and keep it light.

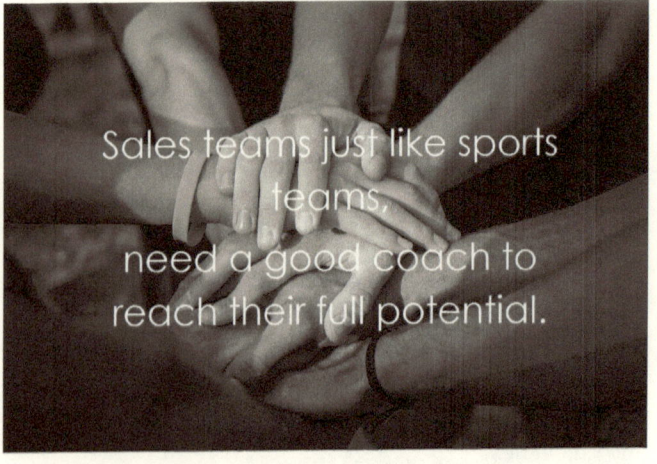

CHAPTER 10

Art of Introductory Email

'There is no formula for the perfect email – Authentic and honest messaging works.' Unknown

In today's marketplace, the email is a very important tool for selling. Before and after the meeting with clients, use the email at the fullest. Before visiting the client, always fix up your meeting schedule on an email and after each meeting, thank the client on the email for his valuable time with the required information.

> Email is the greatest thing. – Wally Amos

I am sharing few sample formats for Email writing for Scheduling a Meeting

Sample Email 1:

Dear Sir

I am from XY company and we are dealing in this product range. This equipment is very useful for your company.

Please find attached the product brochure for your reference.

As discussed we are meeting on 20th March 2017 at your office.

Thanks and Regards

ABC

Sample Letter 2: After the Meeting

Dear Sir

I am highly thankful for your kind courtesy extended during our recent meeting for the discussion on this product.

Find attached the required details.

I will call you day after tomorrow to schedule a meeting to take it further.

Regards

ABC

Sample Email 3: For meeting reconfirmation

Dear Sir

I am thankful for your kind courtesy extended. As scheduled, I look forward to seeing you on ----Date at ----Time.

Thanks & Regards

ABC

Sample Email 4: For a Reference from A Customer

Dear Sir

I am highly thankful to you for referring XYZ for our equipment.

I met them personally and provided them the required information. You may also get the call for the utility and benefits you are getting from the product.

I will keep you updated and thank you once again for helping us with a good reference.

Thanks and Regards

AMC

> 'An Email can make or break a potential opportunity for you, so send and respond to them wisely.' – Leila Lewis

Important points to be considered before writing an email:

1. Subject: Subject should be clear, meaningful and catchy.
2. The email should be short and crisp.
3. There should be no grammatical mistake. The spelling mistake gives wrong impression.

4. The name of the person should be right to whom we are addressing the email.
5. Always add a brochure with your email. It provides the required information to the client.
6. Always close your letter with a positive note and an action plan.
7. You can mention the benefits of your product in the mail. Highlight those points with bullet points.
8. Be specific in your email writing and focus on the target.
9. Never overcommit in your email or never make false promises in your email.
10. Never show rudeness or negativity in your email writing.
11. Be kind in your email.
12. Always apply spell check to your email.

CHAPTER 11

Objection Handling in Sales

MASTERING THE "GAME OF SELLING"

'An objection is not Rejection; it is simply a request for more information' - Bo Bennett

The first objection we face that your price is too high. We are planning for product or equipment that is available at low cost and we are using such equipments. My question to you is that have you ever experienced that someone says that your product price is low. You must ask for little higher price?

Zig Zigler has best explained about how to handle customer objections.

When customer say to you your price is too high. It is better to understand with him and explain to him that are you considering the cost or price. Let me explain to you, A customer would like to buy a Mixer Grinder, the price of branded mixer grinder was Rs 6500. He went to another shop to get the Mixer Grinder at Rs 3500. After three months, he spends Rs 500 on Jar, the cost come down to Rs 4000. After three months motor failure happened and the cost of replacement was another Rs 800. These Mixer grinder cost him Rs 4800 and so on....

It is price or is it cost. Price is a one-time thing, cost is lifetime thing. Don't you want the best lowest possible cost? Always ask for key insightful questions.

When you faced objection that your price is too high, you need to ask mental interpret question, this questions create interest and you can share the comparison of cheap vs quality product.

Prepare comparison in front of customer, keeps customer engaging. Price is one time thing and cost is life time thing.

TCO: total cost of ownership. Total cost of owning something for long time

For example, if you buy a low-cost quality TV as compared to best quality TV. The picture quality will vary and secondly the life of picture tube varies.

Prepare the cost comparison. The lowest price product per month cost will be very high.

People can beat us on price but on one can beat us on cost.

Can I get better price: I am thankful to Victor Antonio about finding way on discount. Every time customer say give me best price and every time customer will say to you that you can do better. When you give away discount you devalue your product, if you really believe that your product is so valuable you never give discount. If you give discount every time, the customer will ask for discount. Customer also thinks that Why he didn't give me discount before? It means that's not the best price. You think that discounting strategy is helping you to close cases. Many time it backfire.

Seven ways to close on pricing objection:

Better price: I have offered you the better price. What you don't want we can eliminate and recalculate the price.

Present option: good better best, instead of the best product why don't you opt for the better product. Scale down versions.

Find a way to offer the substitute.

Another strategy you can sell demo equipment. We have few equipments in our demo fleet or manufactured last year.

Offer a free service: You can offer free service or offer maintenance support.

Offer them a gift: Like screen protector with phone or you can offer them free of cost parts required for service, etc.

Financial option: Why don't we give you payment option of credit period? Give them better interest rate.

Sometimes, we say if I will not give discount I will lose the deal.

You need to ask something in return. If I provide you discount what I can expect something from you. You can ask for more quantity. Provide me good reference.

Next time, if someone asks discount you must ask something in return.

The bestselling style: How people buy, what is the bestselling style? Is it the introvert or the extrovert who sells better? We know that salesperson should be an extrovert; they are great talkers and great closer. They convince the customer.

Introvert is the great listeners but not great closers. Keep this in mind the introvert are short on communicating the values.

There is no study that proves that if you are introvert and you cannot be successful in selling.

Adam Grand is the Professor at University of Peninsula. He started by studying the personality test of 300 people. He tracked the introvert and extrovert. Introvert sold $120 per hour, the extrovert sold $125 per hour. The sale people who were in the middle they sold $145 per hour. The band in the middle sold better. They are called ambirverts.

Introverts are good at listening, extroverts are good in communication and ambirverts are the best of both worlds. They are good in listening and communicating values.

Many years ago, I know one salesperson named Vimal. Vimal was ambivert, he never pushed customers for purchase, he always guided them for sales decision.

If the company says we need a go getter and an extrovert. What is the ideal profile of the salesperson for your market?

Sales influences: We talk about why people buy. One comment every customer say, let me think about it, we will get back to you. You can ask what would be the good time to speak or visit to you. When they say they think about it, what you think they will think about it, there is 8 sec of memory they will forget what you explain. You need to write the feature, in 24 hours people forget 75% of what just said. When I can get back to you. You get back within a week and must note that customer forget 75% of the content. As per my experience you must close the deal on the same day.

In 30 days, the customer will forget 90% what you said and they only retains 5% of the information you conveyed to them. What you do when customer, says we need to think about it? Mr. Customer, it means you are not interested and or not sure about this product. It is one of the reasons. Which is it? If customer says I am interested that I am interested but not sure.

You are done, it means you miss something in the presentation. You gonna say the following. You are not sure of the one reason.

Fit: Is this product is the right fit. Does this product is not adding value.

Functionality: Does it have all the features? It is unique.

Finance: Is there the finance issue? Now, we know this is the money. You need to solve the finance issue. Most people don't like to admit that they have money issue.

One big sale mistake: The majority of companies don't have sales process. In small business, 9 out of 10 don't have sales process. Companies are spending money on offices and marketing.

The requirement is sales process. You need to spend your energy and money on sales process.

If you don't have a sales process, you are just guessing and closing the sale.

I don't believe in script. It is the outliner what I need to say. When I use the script my closing increased and start believing in myself.

You do the presentation you start changing the process…

You must know what to say, when to say and how to say…

Majority of companies don't have a sales process, it's a presentation process…it's about first meeting to calling and then mailing to prospects. It is about followup. What you say what you do when meeting with prospects.

What to introduce first to create the impact. The customer says that I need this product. You need to create the sense of urgency…

You need to do the reverse engineering....knowing what to introduce first...

How you can increase the revenue, cost of operation and market share...

What your equipment can do for them.

Unless the brain experience the pain it will not change.

If you cannot create brain pain, you are fail to create the requirement of your product.

How much money, how much market share they are losing if they are not using my product?

You are not quantifying the value.....

It is more important to have the presentation process.... you want to move towards value conversation...a value conversation you need to quantify the value of your products... The value your product can add to their operation and business.

CHAPTER 12

Pareto Law

What is Pareto Law? How it is applicable to Sales?

Pareto Law is 80/20 rule...Which says 20% of sales team generates 80% of the business. It states that in every walk of life 80% of the effects come from 20% of the causes.

'This law is based on the name of Italian economist Vilfredo Pareto.'

It means our 80% sales team just performed at average level. Their income is average, their performance is average, their sale numbers are average...Why it is so?

What are the reasons for average results of sales professionals?

It is very necessary to understand this behaviour...why sales people are failing in Sales...We need to analyse their behaviour.

What is the root cause for failure or average sales?

In sales, we need to understand in today's economic condition and fast changing economies. Business will come to you, you need to step out to reach the potential buyers and you need to prove your credibility to get the get the business. Sale in not an easy field…To be successful in sales, you have to have positive attitude, your own commitment and organised way of working.

Sales people are failing because they are not committed; their attitude is non-caring towards customers. They think that customer will call them back when they need the products. They feel customer will buy from them only. They are not building close relationship with customer. Lack of service support, slow response to customer needs are the root causes of failure or average performances.

A good sales organisation evaluates its sales team from time to time and upgrades the skills of sales executives to match the market requirements.

Many times, a sales team fails due to very high targets assigned to them. The management assigns targets based on their expectation without involving the ground level sales team. This leads to dissatisfaction among sales team. The sales team think that whatever you do, you will not be able to achieve the sale targets. Then why work so hard when you know that you cannot achieve these targets.

Not recognising the performing sales team: Some time management does not recognise the performance of sales professionals or team. That leads to dissatisfaction among the team.

What successful sales executive are doing to achieve the targets: They are very committed to their profession, they are ethical and they have sense of urgency and the ownership for closing the sales. The most important is that they are very good in follow up.

They are in regular touch with prospect…they continuously visit the customer sites or office to build confidence and relationship. When you are in regular touch with customer and responding to their needs they will believe in you. It create confidence in their mind. The successful salesman are proactive they respond to customer very fast and believe in caring for customer.

CHAPTER 13

Time Management in Selling

Time Management is very important in sales management. Successful people are good in time management. They recognise the value of time management. They know by managing their time well. They can manage their life well. Without time management you cannot manage your life well.

What you want to achieve in your life? Time Management is very closely related to Goals. Your Goals direct you for time management.

The key to time management is self-discipline. What you want to achieve in your life? What you want to be? What are your relationship goals? What makes you exceptional? What make you happy and content in life?

Goals: Top 3% in every field have goals. They have written goals for family and personal development.

Make a list for time management: The successful person thinks in terms of minute. 70% of people are not aware how to manage time. Keep a time log and analyse how you are managing your time. Keep measuring your time. Analyse that your time is paying off as per your goals in your life.

S.No	Time	Action Plan	Comments	Your evaluation
1	9:00 – 9:30			

Set Priority for time Management: Set your priority in life for day-to-day work. Take care for your big rocks in life. We all are aware about the story of managing the life goals and professional goals.

Plan for your monthly calendar for managing the time well.

Average sales person work 90 minutes a day as per research based on California University. Sales person start the day with coffee, newspaper and then few call…then coffee/tea then gossiping with colleagues…

How many minutes you spend with customers? 80-90% of the prospects never heard you? Never heard about your product. Customers are outside the office: If you spend your time in office then the business will be low. How much time you spend face to face with your customer decide the market for your product.

One of the Sales Manager calls the sales meeting & ask what you have not seen in the office, everyone look around. He said that one cannot see any customer in the office so just move out to the field to meet with customer.

In one of the companies they come out with a strategy: They decide that the sales people will go out and spend more face to face time with customer and if customer will say no to them they will be entitle for a free Lunch coupon scheme. Who will get first 10 No/ Rejection will get one lunch coupon free. As a result people started calling & meeting prospects to complete 10 rejections in a day to win a free lunch coupon. At the end of the month some interesting results came out. The company achieved the highest sale ever. To get the 10 rejection in a day sales people calls to more than 300 prospects and 20% of them shown positive interest in their products and later converted into the sales.

We have nature to do the urgent task first and we keep on lingering the important but not urgent work.

Take a task and divide into small pieces. You cannot eat elephant at one go. You can eat it if you cut it into small pieces.

What are the qualities of successful people: They always set priorities for important work in life.

They align their work on below table and focus on important work.

Important & Urgent	Important
Urgent	Less Important and Less Urgent

Concentration: You need to concentrate on one thing at a time and complete it with your 100%.

Parkinson Law: Explain the time management well. Work expands to the time available. If work is of 1 day and you have 2-3 days with you then you will complete your work in 3 days. The best example is the home work given to your kids in summer vacation. They always complete it in last 2-3 days.

Most people are time wasters. In office few people just come for gossiping, they just move from one bench to another for chatting and wasting of your time.

The sales personnel should not waste his time on office gossiping, smoking, chit chatting and drinking tea/coffee. A good sales professional values his time and attach value tag to his time.

He never wastes his time on non-value adding activities.

Deadline and Rewards: Set the deadline and rewards to your time management. Set specific rewards for your every achievement. Set the Goals with positive date and rewards...

Delegate you non-useful work: For successful time management you need to start delegating the non-productive jobs. Spend your time for high-priority job. Delegation requires clarity.

Rules for delegating the job:

Think: Is this job is worth of my time or only I can do it. Think is this job can be delegated for better utilisation of my time.

Right Person: Decide who the right person to complete this job is. Delegate the job to the person who has the required ability to perform the job well.

Make a crystal clear target: Assign the crystal clear target to the team for better focus and productivity.

Time Check: Keep a time check on the assigned task.

Most important part is never assume that work will be completed without followup.

Key Management principal: Key result areas. You have been hired to achieve results...Why am I on the pay role...

MASTERING THE "GAME OF SELLING"

What results are expected from me?

What results are required for my promotion?

Core function/Goals of my job: In the United States, people are not aware what the organisation is expecting from them? They are not clear about their roles.

Key result areaKeep clear channel communication with your boss.

Learning Curve: At first time, you take more time...you can decrease the time by 80%

Priority: Make priority

Name	Priority 1	Priority 2	Priority

Cleanliness: The clean desk, workplace or computer screen plays more important role. The Japanese focus on 5S Principle for the productivity and housekeeping. They always insist which is not important on your desk or not relevant for you then move it to trash box. Keep the task only at the table as per priority.

The area of Focus: Your handbag should be clean and neat, your laptop screen should be neat, etc.

Get up early in the morning. You do the entire day work in just 2-3 hrs. If you need to submit the important reports or proposal, the morning time is the right time to complete the job.

Learn more: If you want to earn more you should learn more, spend one hour every day to invest in you....Driving and travelling time can be utilised for listening audio book or podcast. Convert you're driving or travelling time to educate yourself and get the degree every 4 years...

Utilise your lunch and tea time effectively: An average person wastes lots of time during lunch and tea breaks... you need to start utilising lunch and tea time to increase your knowledge.

Telephone: Telephone is business equipment. There should be rules to manage calls...How I can help you. Use phone call as meeting on wire.

Suggestions for Time Management in Selling:

1. Spend your time for A class or hot prospect first. They are low hanging fruit. Grab the order from them. Then spend your time on B class or warm prospect. They will become your A class prospects in the coming time.
2. Through your behaviour, talking and action, your customers know that you respect their and your own time.
3. Always reach for an appointment at the scheduled time. Call your prospect again in advance that you will be there on the scheduled time.
4. Keep the time for follow-up. In the sales profession, follow-up is the key to get orders and building relationship with the prospects.
5. Invest your time for order generation.

www.ingramcontent.com/pod-product-compliance
Lightning Source LLC
Chambersburg PA
CBHW031054180526
45163CB00002BA/832